SpringerBriefs in Economics

AF182129

For further volumes:
http://www.springer.com/series/8876

Rongxing Guo

Introduction to Intercultural Economics

Springer

Rongxing Guo
Regional Science Association of China
Peking University
Beijing
People's Republic of China

ISSN 2191-5504 ISSN 2191-5512 (electronic)
ISBN 978-3-642-29275-0 ISBN 978-3-642-29276-7 (eBook)
DOI 10.1007/978-3-642-29276-7
Springer Heidelberg New York Dordrecht London

Library of Congress Control Number: 2012935722

© The Author(s) 2012
This work is subject to copyright. All rights are reserved by the Publisher, whether the whole or part of the material is concerned, specifically the rights of translation, reprinting, reuse of illustrations, recitation, broadcasting, reproduction on microfilms or in any other physical way, and transmission or information storage and retrieval, electronic adaptation, computer software, or by similar or dissimilar methodology now known or hereafter developed. Exempted from this legal reservation are brief excerpts in connection with reviews or scholarly analysis or material supplied specifically for the purpose of being entered and executed on a computer system, for exclusive use by the purchaser of the work. Duplication of this publication or parts thereof is permitted only under the provisions of the Copyright Law of the Publisher's location, in its current version, and permission for use must always be obtained from Springer. Permissions for use may be obtained through RightsLink at the Copyright Clearance Center. Violations are liable to prosecution under the respective Copyright Law.
The use of general descriptive names, registered names, trademarks, service marks, etc. in this publication does not imply, even in the absence of a specific statement, that such names are exempt from the relevant protective laws and regulations and therefore free for general use.
While the advice and information in this book are believed to be true and accurate at the date of publication, neither the authors nor the editors nor the publisher can accept any legal responsibility for any errors or omissions that may be made. The publisher makes no warranty, express or implied, with respect to the material contained herein.

Printed on acid-free paper

Springer is part of Springer Science+Business Media (www.springer.com)

Preface

Since the end of the Cold War and, to a lesser extent, even a long time before, a series of global and regional economic issues have been puzzling both theorists and practitioners. They include such important problems as: Why have nations with same or similar natural endowments and political contexts had so different economic performances? Why have trade and economic cooperation been efficient between some nations but more and more difficult between the others? These issues are very crucial to contemporary policymakers and practitioners, and many nice theories have been constructed in order to assess them. Unfortunately, it is argued that most existing theories cannot be used to deal with the above issues satisfactorily.

This book sets out to present an introduction to the analysis of intercultural economic issues that could be misinterpreted by existing theories. It identifies various cultural conditions under which economic policies can (or cannot) be optimized and/or optimally implemented during the process of economic globalization. Another target of this book is to develop new methods and techniques by which to improve the efficiency of intercultural trade and economic cooperation.

This book is an updated excerpt of my larger research project on intercultural economics. The complete version of this research can be found in the book entitled *Intercultural Economic Analysis—Theory and Method* (Springer New York, 2009). Its on-line version can be previewed at the publisher's website:

http://www.springerlink.com/content/978-1-4419-0848-3

I have benefited from many experts and reviewers. They are Chalongphob Sussangkarn (Thailand Development Research Institute and EADN Coordinator), Chia Siow Yue (Singapore Institute for International Affairs), Shigeyuki Abe (Doshisha University), Eui-Gak Hwang (Korea University), David Lim (Griffith University), Steven Pressman (Monmouth University), Ammar Siamwalla (Thailand Development Research Institute), Josef T. Yap (Philippines Institute for Development Studies), Zhang Yunling (Chinese Academy of Social Sciences) as well as a number of anonymous reviewers.

Publishing with Springer has definitely become an integral part of my on-going research on intercultural economics. I have benefited from the innovative jobs done by editors, reviewers and readers at Springer's Beijing, Heidelberg and New York offices during the period when the manuscript was prepared and revised. Toby Chai (Publishing Editor), Barbara Fess (Editor of Economics and Business) and Jon Gurstelle (Senior Editor of Economics and Policy) merit particular mention. Without their help and encouragement, this project could not have been accomplished—at least not in its present form. But all views, drawbacks and errors in this book certainly are mine.

Qiaozi, Beijing, 20 Febrauary 2012 Rongxing Guo

Contents

Chapter 1
Civilizations and Cultures

Abstract This chapter investigates the origins and the evolutions of ancient civilizations of the world. In order to answer why ancient civilizations are only associated with the rivers of the Euphrates, the Tigris, the Nile, the Indus, and the Yellow instead of the others, a challenge-and-response model of cultural development is founded, and the relationship between different natural disasters (threats) and the developments of ancient civilizations is examined. My discussion takes into account of the world's major primary civilizations and concludes that rivers and their cyclic nature of annual floods—not tectonic plate boundaries and earthquakes, tsunamis and volcanic eruptions—were a greater catalyst to the birth of the world's oldest civilizations. This chapter also answers question such as why existing cultures are conflicting and also complementary.

Keywords Ancient civilization · Culture · Cultural evolution · Cultural dynamics · Natural disaster · River system · River flood

1.1 The Origin of Civilizations

Far before the prehistoric period, men had left their footprints on every continent of the world. However, the world's greatest ancient civilizations (such as the Mesopotamian, the Egyptian, the Indus, and the Chinese) were found only in the northern Africa, Middle East, and South and East Asia but not in the rest of the world.

In August 2008, *Geoarchaeology* published an article titled "Tectonic Environments of Ancient Civilizations in the Eastern Hemisphere" (Force 2008, pp. 644–653), which was selected by the *Science* magazine as "The Top 10 ScienceNOWs of 2008" on 24 December 2008 (see Fig. 1.1).

R. Guo, *Introduction to Intercultural Economics*, SpringerBriefs in Economics,
DOI: 10.1007/978-3-642-29276-7_1, © The Author(s) 2012

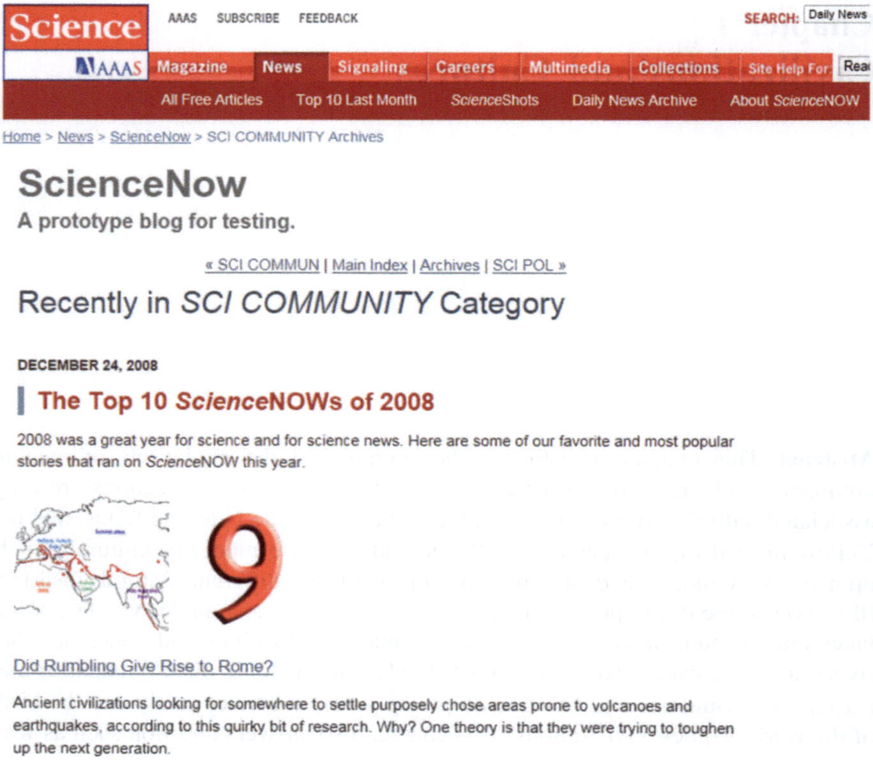
Science
AAAS SUBSCRIBE FEEDBACK
SEARCH: Daily News
AAAS
Magazine | News | Signaling | Careers | Multimedia | Collections | Site Help For | Rea
All Free Articles | Top 10 Last Month | *Science*Shots | Daily News Archive | About *Science*NOW

Home > News > ScienceNow > SCI COMMUNITY Archives

ScienceNow
A prototype blog for testing.

« SCI COMMUN | Main Index | Archives | SCI POL »

Recently in *SCI COMMUNITY* Category

DECEMBER 24, 2008

The Top 10 *Science*NOWs of 2008

2008 was a great year for science and for science news. Here are some of our favorite and most popular stories that ran on *Science*NOW this year.

9

Did Rumbling Give Rise to Rome?

Ancient civilizations looking for somewhere to settle purposely chose areas prone to volcanoes and earthquakes, according to this quirky bit of research. Why? One theory is that they were trying to toughen up the next generation.

Fig. 1.1 The Top 10 ScienceNOWs of 2008 (*Source* http://sciencenow.sciencemag.org/cgi/content/full/2008/822/3)

According to Force's research, earthquake-prone areas along the edges of tectonic plates were, at least in Asia and Europe, far more likely to give birth to the great ancient civilizations than the less dynamic landscapes. The findings were so popular that they immediately received attentions from many world-class magazines and news agencies (see, for example, ScienceNOW Staff 2008; Malakoff 2008; Reebs 2008, and Britannica Online Encyclopedia 2009). Moreover, they have even been selected as study materials in high-school classrooms (see Box 1.1 at the end of this chapter).

However, Force's theory has left the birth of some major ancient civilizations, including those in Egypt and China, unexplained (Guo 2009). Moreover, it is argued that most of the ancient civilizations considered by Force are not primary civilizations, which could lead to an inconsistent and incomparable analysis.[1]

[1] Note that the developments of almost all derivative civilizations have been, to some extent, influenced by other older civilizations (more details will be discussed in Chap. 2).

Table 1.1 Geographical environments and ancient civilizations

Cultural characteristic	Coastal area	Mountain area	Wetland	Forestland	River valley
Increasing sedentism and high population density	*	–	–	–	**(a)
Social stratification and ranking	–	*	–	–	**
Centralized rule/armed military force	–	*	–	–	**
Numbering and writing system	**(b)	–	–	–	**(b)
Metallurgy and craft specialization	*	–	–	–	**
Trade/exchange networks and luxury and exotic goods	**	–	–	–	**

Notes "**" and "*" denote "strongly positive" and "modestly positive" effects on cultural development, respectively. "–" denotes "not clear". (a) denotes result of close correlation between "increasing sedentism and high population density" and "centralized rule/armed military force". (b) denotes result of close correlation between "numbering and writing system" and "trade/exchange networks and luxury and exotic goods"

Most of the world's great ancient civilizations are centered in river valleys. The Sumerians were located along the Euphrates and the Tigris rivers and their tributaries, and the Egyptians around the Nile. Roots of the ancient Indus civilization originate along the Indus river, and the earliest Chinese dynasties centered their culture on the Yellow river. Not only were rivers used for irrigating crops and daily water needs (such as washing, cooking, and bathing), but societies also relied on the rivers for communication and transportation. Rivers were the major highways in these areas. In summary, some reasons why rivers are important to civilization are as follows:

- River water is diverted for agricultural irrigation, industry, hygiene, and related uses.
- Rivers connect major cities; navigable waters carry trade by ship and barge.
- Some communities depend on the fish that live in or travel along rivers.
- Some rivers carry dissolved minerals and organic compounds.
- Alluvial deposits can form fertile deltas where a river flows into a lake or ocean.

The hydrological characteristics of rivers heavily influenced ancient riparian civilizations. Large workforces were needed to divert water for irrigation and build protective works to minimize flood damage. This led to increasing sedentism, high population density, and the need for a centralized administration along the river valley. The development of "hydraulic societies" in China that were dependent on complex irrigation systems is a good example. The cost of hydraulic construction and its subsequent maintenance required a political and social structure capable of forceful extraction of labor (Wittfogel 1957). Furthermore, with regard to the utilization of water resources in river valleys, upstream communities usually have geographical advantages over downstream residents. As a result, social stratification and armed military forces emerged alongside large-scale water control. These are very important processes in the development of ancient civilizations.

Table 1.1 compares river valley with other types of geographical places (such as coastal area, mountain area, wetland, and forestland) in terms of the suitability for serving as the 'cradle' of ancient civilizations.

In addition, it is reasonable to suppose that the lower reaches of most, if not all, rivers giving birth to ancient civilizations were characterized as wetlands (not suitable for agriculture) during ancient times, especially at the deltas.[2] This, probably, might be the reason why the ancient civilizations originated in the upper (or middle) vis-à-vis the lower reaches (and deltas) of the river valleys. Archaeologists recognize that in some cases, in some places, at some times, simple societies for one reason or the other morph into more and more complex societies, and in the process some become civilizations. The reasons for this are quite controversial, but the characteristics of complexity recognized in ancient civilizations are pretty much agreed upon:

- Natural selection of mankind
- Increasing sedentism and high population density
- Social stratification and ranking
- Numbering and writing system
- Time and calendar
- Centralized rule and/or armed military force
- Control of food as in agriculture or pastoralism
- Craft specialization and metallurgy
- Luxury and exotic goods
- Trade or exchange networks
- Architecture and monumental buildings

Not all of these characteristics necessarily have to be present for a particular cultural group to be considered a civilization, but all of them are considered evidence of relatively complex societies. Still, Table 1.1 does not tell us why there were no ancient civilizations in many river valleys of the world, which include, among others, the Yangtze, Mississippi, Volga, and Rhine. Thus, other major force(s) contributing to the development of ancient civilizations must have been absent there. We can borrow some knowledge from *The Origin of Species by Means of Natural Selection* (Darwin 1859). As many more individuals of each tribe are born than can possibly survive, especially in areas with serious natural disasters and threats and, consequently, there is a frequently recurring struggle for existence, it follows that any being, if it varies, however slightly, in any manner profitable to itself, under the complex and sometimes changing conditions of life, will have a better chance of surviving, and thus will naturally outlive others.

The root of the word disaster comes from the Latin 'aster' meaning 'of the stars'. 'dis' means 'bad or misfortune'. In ancient times, stars were assumed to predict impeding events including bad events. So what they combinedly imply is

[2] Even today, we can still find wetlands at the deltas of the Indus, the Euphrates, the Tigris and the Yellow rivers.

that when the stars are in a bad position a bad event will happen. A natural disaster is an event caused by natural forces that often pose a significant danger to human life or have a significant effect on the property of human beings. Typically, after the disaster, the human populations either are displaced (left homeless) or killed. The resulting loss depends on the capacity of the human population to circumvent or resist the disaster. Although natural hazards have been around ever since the earth came into existence, they will hence never result in damages to human beings in areas without vulnerability (e.g., strong earthquakes in uninhabited areas).[3]

Natural disasters often have economic and emotional effects on people and property directly affected. Environmentally, natural disasters can also be important to local ecosystems. The tragic consequences of natural disasters include death, injuries, loss of clean water, loss of shelter, loss of personal household goods, major population movements, loss of sanitation, loss of routine hygiene, disruption of solid waste management, public concern for safety, increased pests and vectors, damage to health care system, worsening of chronic illnesses, loss of electricity, toxic/hazardous exposure, loss of food supply, and standing surface water (Keim 2007). Having a better understanding of these natural disasters and their influences on human beings can help to better prepare against and perhaps minimize or prevent damages resulting from these disasters. Furthermore, the ability to predict and to combat or prevent natural disasters that threaten human beings is crucial to the formation of human civilizations.

Natural disasters can be classified into two categories—slow and rapid onsets—each of which also includes various sub-types, as the following:

Slow onset

- Deforestation
- Desertification
- Drought
- Epidemic
- Famines (natural)
- Insect infestations

Rapid onset

- Avalanches
- Dust-storms
- Earthquakes
- Extreme temperatures (including cold and heat waves)
- Floods
- Landslides
- Mud-rock flows
- Snow and ice-storms

[3] The term 'natural' has consequently been disputed because the events simply are not hazards or disasters without human involvement.

- Thunderstorms
- Tsunamis
- Volcanoes
- Wildfires
- Windstorms

It is worth noting that some of the above natural disasters are interrelated to each other. For example, landslides and tsunamis are usually the subsequences of earthquakes; droughts are closely related to extreme temperatures; and windstorms are usually followed by floods, landslides, and mud-rock flows in mountain areas caused by floods in river valleys. And, after these disasters, there are often epidemics and virus spreads in the affected areas. Another natural disaster, predators' attack, though no longer crucial to human beings in modern times, played a very important role in the evolution of human life during prehistoric era. Finally, we will compare the following six types of natural disasters as well as their influences on the formation of ancient civilizations:

- Drought
- Earthquake
- Famine (induced by natural force)
- Flood (including levee break of rivers)
- Predators' attack
- Wind storm (including cyclone, hurricane, tornado, tropical storm, snow and ice-storms, dust-storm, thunderstorm, etc.)

1.2 A Theory of Cultural Evolution

Table 1.2 shows the possible effects of six natural disasters and threats (i.e., drought, earthquake, famine, flood, predators' attack and wind storm) on the civilizational development of human beings at prehistoric era. Among all the natural disasters and threats, river flood plays the most important role in the development of ancient civilizations.[4] Obviously, the creation of 'calendar', one of the most important components considered as signs of the birth of a civilization, almost has nothing to do with predators' attack, contagious disease or earthquake. It is, however, closely related to the regularity of 'river flooding'. For instance, in ancient Egypt the 15th day of June, or the start of flooding season of the Nile, was selected as the first day of a new year. In addition, since the natural disasters and threats are more frequently found at river valleys than in the other geographical places (as shown in Table 1.3), men living by river valleys have a more crying

[4] Note that other natural disasters and threats (such as predators' attack) might be most important in the evolution of mankind during the prehistoric period.

Table 1.2 A challenge-response model: natural disasters and ancient civilizations

Cultural characteristic	Drought	Earthquake	Famine (natural)	Flood	Predators' attack	Wind storm
Natural selection of mankind	**	*	**	**	**	*
Control of food as in agriculture or pastoralism	**	–	**	**	–	**
Numbering and writing system	*(a)	–	*(a)	**(a)	–	*(a)
Calendar	*	–	*	**		*
Centralized rule	*	*	**	**	**	–
Architecture and monumental buildings	–	**	–	**	*	*

Notes "**" and "*" denote "strongly positive" and "modestly positive" correlations between a natural disaster (or threat) and cultural evolution, respectively. "–" denotes "not clear" or "uncertain correlations". (a) denotes result of close correlation between "numbering and writing system" and "calendar"

Table 1.3 How natural disasters affect human beings in different geographical areas

Natural disaster (threat)	Coastal area	Mountain area	Wetland	Forestland	River valley
Drought	*	**	–	*	**(a)
Earthquake	**(b)	**(c)	*	*	**(d)
Famine (natural)	–	–	*	–	**
Flood	*	*	*		**(e)
Predators' attack	**	**	**	**	**
Wind storm	**(f)	*(g)	*	–	**(e)

Notes "**" and "*" denote "most serious" and "modestly serious" damages to human beings, respectively. "–" denotes "not clear". (a) more serious in upper than in lower reaches. (b) includes tsunami and other related disasters. (c) includes unpredictable landslide and other disasters. (d) includes unpredictable levee break and other related disasters, especially at lower reaches. (e) more serious in lower than in upper reaches. (f) mainly includes cyclone, hurricane, tornado, tropical storm, thunderstorm and other related disasters. (g) usually includes snow and ice-storms, predictable mud-rock flow and other related disasters

need to develop various scientific methods and technological tools in order to survive than those living in the other places (Gelles 2000).[5]

Around the world, unruly rivers have long driven a hard bargain. In exchange for rich soil, irrigated land, and convenient transportation, they toiled the flood-plain dwellers to deal with an occasional washout. A level of sediment consistent with a flood has been found in many parts of Mesopotamia and in some other parts of the world. Like most other Genesis stories, the flood account is found in more places than just Genesis. For example, the following, flood-related story is included in the Testament:

5 Other literature in this regard would include Wittfogel (1957), Worsher (1985), and Scarborough (2003).

> In the 600th year of Noah's life, in the second month, on the 17th day of the month, on the same day all the fountains of the great deep burst open, and the floodgates of the sky were opened. And the rain fell upon the land for 40 days and forty nights. On the very same day Noah and Shem and Ham and Japheth, the sons of Noah, and Noah's wife and the three wives of his sons with them, entered the ark, they and every beast after its kind, and all the cattle after their kind, and every creeping thing that creeps on the land after its kind, and every bird after its kind, all sorts of birds. So they went into the ark to Noah, by twos of all flesh in which was the breath of life. And those that entered, male and female of all flesh, entered as God had commanded him; and the Lord closed it behind Him. Then the flood came upon the land for 40 days; and the water increased and lifted up the ark, so that it rose above the land. And the water prevailed and increased greatly upon the land; and the ark floated on the surface of the water. And the water prevailed more and more upon the land, so that all the high hills everywhere under the sky were covered. The water prevailed fifteen cubits higher, and the hills were covered. And all flesh that moved on the land perished birds and cattle and beasts and every swarming thing that swarms upon the land, and all mankind; of all that was on the dry land, all in whose nostrils was the breath of the spirit of life, died. Thus He blotted out every living thing that was upon the face of the land, from man to animals to creeping things and to birds of the sky, and they were blotted out from the land; and only Noah was left, together with those that were with him in the ark. And the water prevailed upon the land one hundred and 50 days. (Genesis, 7:11–24)

The worldwide extent of sedimentary evidence for the flood compares favorably with most of the geologic epochs. Legends found in numerous geographically separated cultures worldwide that converge, with minor variation, upon the biblical account of the great flood. Converging accounts of an ancient Island paradise lost in a massive deluge are found in the Greek and Egyptian legends of Atlantis, Sumerian tale of Dilmun, the Babylonian Nibiru, and ancient Chinese and Indian legends. Some examples are as follows: the cities of Heliki and Boura, Greece, sunk into the sea following an earthquake in 373 BC; ruins of submerged cities at Olous, Crete; Carpia, Iberia, and many others have been identified. Vast ancient ruins have been found off the coast of cities like Alexandria, Egypt. A sunken city just west of Cuba and east of the Yucatan contains megaliths "of a kind you'd find at Stonehenge or Easter Island," large structures that "bear a remarkable resemblance to the pyramidal design of Mayan and Aztec temples in Mexico," and "symbols and inscriptions" in a language that has not yet been identified (Stewart 2008).

While these discoveries individually and collectively do not serve as 'proof' of a great flood, exploration of the world produced increasing evidence that terrible floods had, in fact, occurred throughout the world. High mountains demonstrated geological scoring and drift materials demonstrating that they had been covered by rapid floodwaters. In "The Case for the Flood" in *Forbidden History*, Bros (2005, pp. 44–5) describes:

> As explorers started to bring home descriptions of the world from afar, science was horrified to see a picture emerging of a planet scarred by massive movements of water, generally from the northwest to the southeast, over its surface. The northwestern sides of whole mountains were scored as if they had been subjected to fast-moving waters containing gravel and boulders. Floodwater was unmistakably the source of the scoring because science could see the same effect from fast-moving rivers. Furthermore, those same sides of the mountains were also home to massive buildups of drift materials, detritus presumably left behind by receding waters. Again, this was an effect that mimicked natural

actions in the real world. These drift deposits even contained the remains of animals, including the woolly mammoth.

The development of the ancient Chinese civilization along the valley of the Yellow river provides even stronger evidence to support the hypothesis that civilization originates as a human response to river floods. China has had a particularly long and terrible history of devastating flooding. More than five thousand kilometers long, the Yellow river begins much high above sea level in the Western mountain area and ends at the Yellow Sea. During the long history of China, the Yellow river has been dubbed as "China's Sorrow," because it has killed more people than any other river in the world (Sinclair 1987). At the same time, the river has also been known as the "cradle of Chinese civilization" and considered a blessing with a nickname "China's Pride". The events which occurred in the Yellow river during the ancient times have accounted for the major part of cultural formation in ancient China. For example, the following are reported in the classic of Chinese history:

- c. twenty-first century BC, floods caused numerous deaths within the valley of the Yellow river; a minister was appointed by Shun, a legendary emperor in China, to take preventive measures after a disastrous flood, but to little avail, because there was another great flood a few years later. The minister was banished, and his son, named Yu (or Dayu, great Yu), was appointed to control the river floods. Great Yu came up with the idea of dredging the river to encourage the water to flow in its proper channel.
- c. 1988 BC, great Yu's son, named Qi, succeeded to the throne of the Xia dynasty.
- c. 1551 BC, Shang dynasty was established in the lower reaches of the Yellow river, a place exposed to serious floods.
- c. 1312 BC, to avoid natural disasters resulting from the floods of the Yellow river, the Shang court conducted its fifth, and the last, move of its capital from Yan (today's Qufu city of Shandong province) to Yin (today's An'yang city of Henan province).
- c. 1046 BC, Zhou dynasty was established in Hao (near today's Xi'an) in the upper reaches of Yellow river.
- 770 BC, the Zhou court moved its capital to Luoyi (today's Luoyang city of Henan province in the upper-middle reaches of Yellow river.
- c. 600 BC, Laozi was born at Luyi of today's Henan province, who, after having spent most of his occupational career in Luoyi, found Taoism.
- 551 BC, Confucius was born in Qufu at the lower reaches of Yellow river; he found Confucianism. Though contradicted each other in many aspects, including the ways of flood control, Confucianism and Taoism have encompassed the most important elements of Chinese culture.
- 372 BC, Mencius was born in Tengzhou at the lower reaches of Yellow river. Known as the second sage of Confucianism, Mencius criticized the egocentric flood-control measures taken by the upstream states. The following is an example:

> Baigui [a minister of the state of Wei in today's Henan province] said, 'My management of the waters is superior to that of Yu.' Mencius replied, 'You are wrong, Sir. Yu's regulation of the waters was according to the natural laws of water. He, therefore, made the four seas their receptacle, while you make the neighboring states their receptacle. Water flowing out of its channels is called an inundation. The inundating waters are disastrous to the neighboring states, and what a benevolent man detests. You are wrong, my dear Sir!'[6]

During the Chinese history, attempts to control the Yellow river have been categorized by different strategic approaches. One strategy is the active control of the river: to confine it within a narrow channel by high levees. The narrow-channel concept carries the danger of active erosion of the levee, but it encourages the fast flow that keeps sediment in suspension, and therefore, allows only slow silting of the river bed: in some circumstances the river may actually cut its bed deeper. However, there is little reserve capacity for absorbing a major flood crest, and even the high levees will inevitably be overtopped. On the other hand, one might adopt a strategy of confining the river in a wider flood plain, between lower levees. This is cheaper to construct, but requires that more land be sacrificed to river control. It also permits a slower flow, and promotes silt deposition. Over time the river will inevitably build up its bed. However, there is much more reserve capacity for flood water in a wide channel, and there is room to build small diversion dams to keep the river course to the center of the channel, avoiding the problem of scouring against the levee foundations.

Although Confucianism and Taoism are similar to each other in the sense that they want peace and good behavior, there are many differences between the two schools of thought. More often than not, Chinese scholars have seen the close confinement of the river as a "Confucian" solution of discipline and order imposed upon nature: this contrasts with the "Taoist" solution of allowing the river a more "natural" course within lighter constraints. In either case, however, river engineering represented a tremendous interference with any "natural" regime; and the contrasting solutions were more accurately characterized as being opposites of engineering than philosophical approaches. Certainly, these contradicting phenomena are the defining results of the differing living conditions on which Confucian and Taoist founders were based (see Table 1.4). Specifically, the Confucians, including Confucius and Mencius and early followers, all of whom lived within the lower reaches of the Yellow river, had either suffered more seriously from river floods, or been more deeply impressed by such flood-related stories as told by their elders, than Laozi, the founder of Taoism. For example, the following story is included in the analects of Mencius (372–289 BC):

> In the time of Emperor Yao [about the twenty-second century BC], the waters, flowing out of their channels, inundated the Central Kingdom. Snakes and dragons occupied it, and the people had no place in which they could settle themselves. In the low grounds they made nests for themselves on the trees or raised platforms, and in the high grounds they made

---

[6] Cited from Mencius (c. 300 BC, Gaozi II).

Table 1.4 Confucianism versus Taoism: Some basic facts

	Confucianism	Taoism
Founder's name	Kongzi (Confucius)	Laozi (Lao Tzu)
Founder's year of birth	551 BC	c. 600 BC
Founder's place of birth/living	Qufu—lower reaches of Yellow river	Luyi/Luoyi[a]—middle and upper reaches of Yellow river
How the founder suffered from river flood	Very serious	Not serious
Overall goal	Find peaceful and harmonious place of life	No overall goal
Rule of behavior	Follow a certain relationship between people	Follow the life according to the Tao
Attitude toward flood control	Narrow channel by high levees	Wider flood plain between lower levees

[a] Laozi spent most of his career first at Luoyi (capital of the Eastern Zhou dynasty) and later at the mountain areas in western China

> caves. It is said in the Book of History, 'The waters in their wild course warned me.' Those 'waters in their wild course' were the waters of the great inundation. Emperor Shun dispatched Yu to reduce the waters to order. Yu dug open their obstructed channels, and conducted them to the sea. He drove away the snakes and dragons, and forced them into the grassy marshes. On this, the waters pursued their course through the country, even the waters of the Jiang, the Huai, the He and the Han, and the dangers and obstructions which they had occasioned were removed. The birds and beasts which had injured the people also disappeared, and after this men found the plains available for them.[7]

Subject to their differing living conditions within the valley of the Yellow river, the Confucian and Taoist schools each has its unique view on basic beliefs, overall goals, goals of the individual behavior, view of life, rule of behavior and views of society. For example, the overall goal of the Confucianism is to find a peaceful and harmonious place in life; while that of the Taoism has no overall goal. The Taoists are just set to follow the life according to the Tao, but the Confucians follow a certain behavior and want to be harmony with nature. The Confucians believed that one should be improved by education and development of your character and the need to understand the complicated relationships with your family members, with the government and with the society as a whole, while the Taoists believed that the life they lived with the Tao was good and following the society's ways was bad.

During the past thousands of years, the management of the Yellow river has been at the cost of large amount of physical and human capitals and, consequently, generated various technologies and wisdoms, and created a particular culture. It is noticeable that the Yangtze river, which is even longer than the Yellow river, has also flooded numerous times during the Chinese history. Why was the ancient Chinese civilization found in the valley of the Yellow river instead of that of the

[7] Cited from Mencius (c. 300 BC, Teng Wen Gong II). Note that the term 'dragon', which has also been known as the 'God of water or rain' in traditional Chinese culture, probably was referred as to the beast 'crocodile' or other amphibious lizards.

Yangtze river? The reason might be that during the ancient times most areas of the Yangtze river valley either were wetlands (especially in the lower reaches) or perhaps had no history of terrible floods (especially in the upper reaches). Wetland, unlike an arable land, is not a suitable birthplace for a civilization; and the cyclic nature of the annual flood of rivers can provide the necessary conditions under which a civilization grows to an advanced stage at river valleys (as suggested in Table 1.2).

The following case also is different from that of the Yellow river. Beginning as a trickle in northern Minnesota, and flowing nearly 4,000 km south to the Gulf of Mexico, the Mississippi draws water from thousands of tributaries across 31 states and two Canadian provinces. The Mississippi river valley is one of the world's most fertile valleys. Flooding is nothing new for the Mississippi, which has regularly overrun its banks for tens of thousands of years. Originally, the waters of the Mississippi spread over many thousand square miles of lowlands. Unlike cultivated farmland, wetlands or marshes possess a sponge-like quality that absorbs excess water in times of flooding. On the basis of the assumptions illustrated in Tables 1.1 and 1.2, we may conclude that probably it was the lack of unruly rivers (to generate regular flooding) and/or of riverside land suitable to agriculture that did not give birth to great ancient civilizations in the Americas.[8]

Indeed, the Yellow river is the most important dummy to explain the differences between the Chinese culture and the other cultures in the rest of the world. The changes of the river's course have been spectacular, and the river mouth has sometimes changed catastrophically by hundreds of kilometers. It has had dozens of major and numerous minor changes in course during the past thousands of years, each leading to great amount of not only human casualties but also property losses. Much of the problem stems from the high silt content of the river. Millions of tons of yellow mud choke the channel, causing the river to overflow and change course. Water is held in by dikes of ever increasing height. In its lower reaches, the riverbed has actually become 20 m higher than the level of the surrounding countryside. All these features have largely decided the lifestyle of the Chinese people, especially of those with close proximity to the Yellow river.

For example, after having compared the architectures of the Yellow river valley and of southeast provinces (such as Guangdong and Fujian), we can find that the houses and other buildings at the Yellow river valley, especially at the lower reaches of the Yellow river, were much simpler and, of course, less firm in structure, with almost no valuable materials. Since most of the Han population living in the southeast provinces are descendants of those who immigrated from the Yellow river valley), only geographical feature can explain this difference. People living at the Yellow river valley must have frequently abandoned their homes in order to escape from the unruly, disastrous floodwaters. For example, in

[8] Of course, we still need more detailed archeological evidence in order to support this hypothesis. External influences on the evolutions of ancient civilizations will be discussed in Chap. 2.

the first half of the Shang dynasty, that is, from c. 1551 to c. 1312 BC, China's capital city was moved five times, with an average interval of only about 50 years. This can also explain, at least partially, why ancient China lacked such great architectures and monumental buildings as those that were constructed in ancient Egypt (such as Pyramids) and ancient Rome (such as Colosseum).

The Yellow river can tell us more details about China's history and culture. For example, the difficulties in securing sufficient food within the valley of the Yellow river—probably the result of frequent natural disasters—laid the economical foundations for Chinese cuisine. Unlike the Westerners, the Chinese have a much smaller percentage of fat and meat as the main ingredient in their daily diet. This instantly reminds me of the hypothesis that it is the shortage of food in quantity and category that drove the Chinese to develop many cooking methods (including braising, boiling, braising with soy sauce, roasting, baking, grilling, scalding, deep-frying, steaming, drying, and salt-preserving) in order to *make* their food more delicious. In addition, the scarcity of food has resulted in a special eating habit (i.e., dishes are placed on the center of a table and everybody shares with each other) in ancient China. More often than not, all the above conditions have also contributed to the formation of a collectivistic-style culture in China.

By contrast, since the living condition in Europe (the original place of Western culture) was not so difficult as that in China, it seems quite unnecessary that ancient European people with enough food supplies had to invent some, if not all, of the above cooking methods and to follow the traditional Chinese eating habit. What is more important is, since the Europeans have not met with so many serious natural disasters as in the other places (such as Asia, Middle East and northern Africa) during the civilizational period, it also seems likely that there was not a need for the large-scale mobilizations of manpower in order to deal with such natural disasters as river floods and others. The final result is the birth of a culture focusing on individualism.

1.3 Cultures and Culture Areas

Unlike political and economic factors, cultural factors (such as ethnicity, language, and religion) keep relatively few changes over a comparatively longer period of time. They can, therefore, serve as an important instrument for the comparative analysis of the world economy. However, given the great varieties of ethnic, linguistic, and religious groups throughout the world (see Appendix A for details), the number of individual cultures is too large to be a practical tool and it would be very difficult to conduct useful multicultural economic comparisons.[9]

[9] If X, Y, and Z are used to denote the numbers of ethnic, linguistic, and religious groups, respectively, the largest number of cultures (N) that encompass different kinds of the ethnic, linguistic, and religious groups can be expressed by $N=X \cdot Y \cdot Z$.

Consequently, for ease of facilitating cross-cultural economic analyses and comparisons, our analytical framework will be mainly based on a synthetic term—'culture area'.

The concept of 'culture area' reflects the theoretical position that each culture, on whatever level it may be analyzed, must be examined with regard to its own history and the general principles of independent invention, culture borrowing, cultural integration, and so on. In the *International Encyclopedia of the Social Sciences*, culture areas are defined as 'geographical territories in which characteristic culture patterns are recognizable through repeated associations of specific traits and, usually, through one or more modes of subsistence that are related to the particular environment' (1972, p. 563). There usually exists a small and relatively homogeneous core in each culture area. Culture areas also have boundaries. The influence of a specific culture is always the strongest in the core and becomes weaker from the core to peripheral areas. In theory, the boundary of a culture area can be determined as the line beyond which the influence of culture comes to zero. However, the boundaries between culture areas are not necessarily distinct; recognizable cultures within a given area may contrast with those of neighboring ones, and if the boundaries are not sharply delineated, zones of composite culture or blended traits may make the transition from one to another a matter of gradation. Within a single area, quite different ways of life may coexist as characteristic patterns.

Although distinctions between regions based on culture are as old as mankind, the roots of the culture area concept can be traced to Europe, where the work of the German geographer Friedrich Ratzel (1844–1904) inspired the development of the *Kulturkreise* (cultural circles) school. *Kulturkreise*, which attempted to reconstruct the diffusion, or spread, of cultural traits from a few of dominant cultural clusters, was associated with the German anthropologists Leo Frobenius (1873–1938) and Fritz Graebner (1877–1934). It was not in Europe, however, but in the United States that the concept of culture area gained real social scientific cohesion. One impetus for this development was the need to make sense of the growing body of ethnographic data produced by early anthropological expeditions in the American West.

In 1917, Clark Wissler (1870–1947), an anthropologist with the American Museum of Natural History, used the culture area concept to integrate what was known about Native American communities. Wissler gathered together ethnographic data from a variety of sources and used these data to group Native American tribes based on similarities and differences in their substance systems, modes of transport, textiles, artwork, and religious practice. As a result of this effort, he discerned a distinct geographic pattern, with groups living in proximity, or in similar natural environments, sharing many cultural traits. Wissler eventually defined nine distinct Native American culture areas, grouping tribes that shared significant traits.[10]

---

[10] Cited from Brown (2005).

Even though the pioneer and classic works on the formulation and application of the culture area concept were carried out several decades later (see, for example, Wissler 1917), early studies on classification of culture areas may date back to the late 19th or the very early twentieth century (Driver 1962). In 1896, O.T. Mason recognized 18 culture areas or environments in the Western Hemisphere (Kroeber 1939, p. 7). Farrand (1904) suggested a seven-part classification of North American Indians, including considerations of both geography and culture, and discussed them at some length. Holms (1903) mapped the North American Indians into 19 geo-ethnic groups that correspond well to the groupings in the later work of both Wissler (1917) and Kroeber (1939). Thereafter, there are a number of case studies on the culture area distinctions in Asian and other cultures.[11]

The Culture area concept is a means of organizing a vast amount of variegated ethnographic data into comprehensive units within a classificatory system. It depends on a number of criteria or determinants in the isolation of units. In theory, major considerations in recognizing these areas and sub-areas are ecological zones, patterns of cultural integration and correlations between the independently diffused traits, among others. In practice, however, since the factors by which a culture is determined or influenced are so numerous, the cultural classification of diversified economies in the world is an extremely difficult task. Therefore, it seems necessary to simplify the multicultural division of the world.

While scholars have generally agreed in their identification of the major cultures in history and on those that exist in the world, there have also been differences of opinions. For example, Spengler (1928) specified eight major cultures and McNeil (1963) discussed nine civilizations in the whole history. Bagby (1958, pp. 165–74) saw seven major civilizations or nine if Japan is distinguished from China and the Eastern Orthodox from the West. Rostovanyi (1993) identified seven and Braudel (1994) nine major contemporary civilizations. Quigley (1979, pp. 77 and 88) argued for 16 clear historical cases and very probably eight others, while Toynbee (1961, pp. 546–7) raised the number to 21 or 23.

Such divergent opinions depend in part, as noted by Huntington (1996, p. 44), on whether cultural groups such as the Chinese and Indians are thought to have had a single civilization throughout history or two or more closely related civilizations, one being the offspring of the other. Despite these differences, the identity of the major civilizations is not contested. As Melko (1969, p. 133) argued, there exist at least 12 major cultures in the world, seven of which no longer exist (Mesopotamian, Egyptian, Cretan, Classical, Byzantine, Middle American, and Andean) and five of which still do (Chinese, Japanese, Indian, Islamic, and Western).

From the perspective of intercultural politics, Galtung (1992, pp. 23–4) and Huntington (1996, pp. 45–7) developed a similar multicultural structure of seven or eight culture areas, including:

- Sinic

[11] The earliest literature would include Bacon (1946), Kroeber (1947), Naroll (1950) and Patai (1951).

- Japanese
- Hindu
- Islamic
- Western
- Orthodox
- Latin American and, possibly,
- African[12]

Both Galtung and Huntington defined the Orthodox culture as distinct from its parent Byzantine culture and from Western Christian culture, and maintained that the Japanese culture was also distinct. According to Quigley (1979, p. 83), Japan was, to a large extent, the offspring of the Sinic culture. Alternatively, both should be classified as parts of a larger East Asian culture area.

After taking account of the influences of anthropological differences, Sapper (1968) classified the world into 11 cultural divisions, including

- Germanic
- Latin
- Slavic
- West Asian
- Indian
- East Asian
- The inland
- African
- Malayan
- Australian and
- The North Pole

However, this classification satisfies the anthropologists only. Political economists have usually treated Australia as part of the Western culture area and Malaysia as part of the East (or Southeast) Asian culture area. Other authors have defined a relatively small number of culture areas. For example, Kendall (1976) classified the world into six distinct culture areas, including

- Western
- Islamic
- Indian
- East Asian
- Southeast Asian and
- African

[12] Other authors who advanced similar arguments include Lind (1990); Buzan (1991); Gilpin (1993); Lind (1992, 1994); Rostovanyi (1993); Vlahos (1991); Puchala (1994); Elmandjra (1994) and The Economist (1994, pp. 21–3).

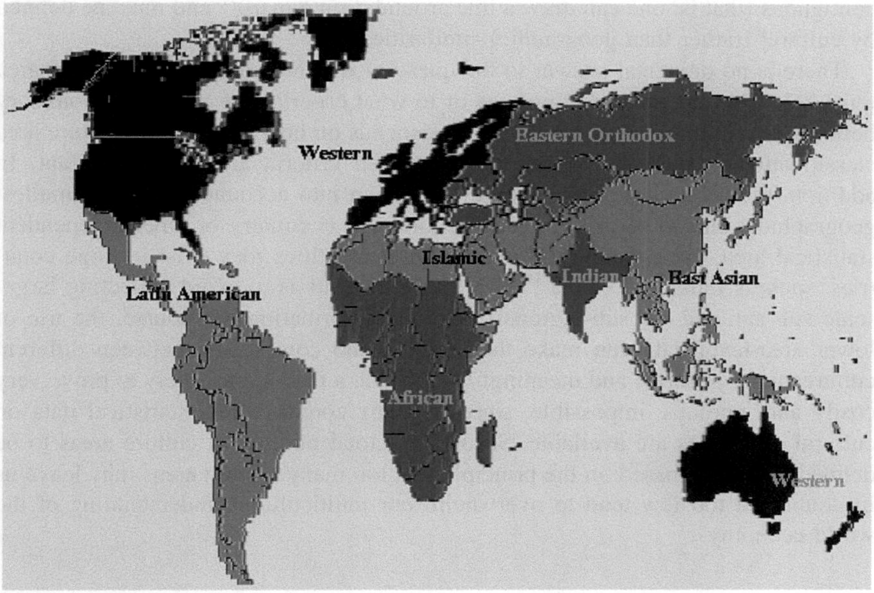

Fig. 1.2 The seven culture areas

In Kendall's study, the Western culture area, which is composed of four sub-culture areas (Northwest Europe, Canada, USA, South Africa, Australia, and New Zealand; the Mediterranean; Central Asia; and the former USSR), is very heterogeneous in terms of geography, political economy, and culture. Quite independently, Aono (1979, pp. 48–51) developed a framework that closely parallels Kendall's (1976) on the salience to a world of six culture areas, including

- East Asian
- Malayan
- South Asian
- Islamic
- African and
- European

Again, the European area is assumed to include at least three economically and geographically heterogeneous cultures (or sub-cultures)—Germanic, Latin, and Slavic.

Generally, the cultural division of the world economy may vary, usually depending on different purposes or criteria as selected by researchers. Our classification of seven contemporary culture areas (i.e., the African, the East Asian, the Eastern Orthodox, the Indian, the Islamic, the Latin American and the Western areas, as shown in Fig. 1.2) is based on the criteria by which a culture area must be contiguous (that is, one can draw a line around it on a map)[13] and must be defined by cultural (rather than geographic) similarities.

There is no universal answer to the question whether similar people in an area must belong to the same culture area or to what criteria that can define boundary between two culture areas. Obviously, it depends on how detailed the culture area classification is intended to be, and on which criteria are most important. In addition, the following principles are also taken into account. First, the smallest geographical unit to be used in each culture area is country or other independent statistical area, even though different cultural identities may exist in large countries, such as India and China.[14] The reason for this is to avoid collecting large-scale sub-national (or sub-regional) data and information. Of course, the use of lower area-level data can make the analysis and comparison between different cultures more accurate and meaningful. But such a task seems likely to prove very costly and, perhaps, impossible, since in many countries few statistical data on cultural minorities are available. Second, the total number of culture areas to be defined should be based on the principle that too many culture areas may leave us in doubt and too few tend to overwhelm our multicultural understanding of the world economy.

1.4 Summary

The geographical characteristics of river systems have heavily influenced the ancient civilizations that grew there. However, why are these ancient civilizations only associated with the rivers of the Euphrates, the Tigris, the Nile, the Indus, and the Yellow instead of the others? In addition, it is also a myth that there were no great ancient civilizations in America. This chapter investigates the origins of and the evolutions of ancient civilizations of the world. Specifically, the relationship between different natural disasters and threats and the developments (evolutions) of existing ancient civilizations will be examined, providing evidence to answer why some river valleys (instead of other types of geographical places) are suitable to serve as the 'cradle' of ancient civilizations. After briefly reviewing the role of the Yellow river in the formation of Chinese culture, this chapter will conduct a brief comparison of two conflicting and complementary theories—Confucianism and Taoism.

Comparative cultural analysis has been widely used by both anthropologists and cultural geographers, primarily because it facilitates comparisons between regions, assists in the historical reconstruction of economic and cultural developments and lends itself to questions about the impact of the natural environment on the form of

[13] The only exception is the Western culture.

[14] For example, Northwest India belongs to the Islamic culture; and the Muslims and Tibetans in Northwest and Southwest China have nothing to do with the Han Chinese culture.

human cultures. The classification of human groups into culture areas has been critiqued on the grounds that the bases for these classifications, such as similar farming systems or pottery styles, are always arbitrary. Despite this limitation, the organization of human communities into cultural areas remains a common practice throughout the social sciences. Since 'culture' and 'area' are both generalized terms, their use in combination gives no real clue as to the precise meaning. When comparing one culture area with another, the level of abstraction must be the same. Although many factors at the base of any recognizable culture area are ecological in nature, the culture area concept is one that conforms to the doctrine of limited possibilities rather than to a simple geographic determination. Viewed in this light and assessed according to the character of the geographic units and the degree of complexity of cultural similarities within, and differences between, units, the culture area concept takes shape as a classificatory device of marked utility in describing the cultural regions of the world.

The definition of culture areas is enjoying a resurgence of practical and theoretical interests as social scientists conduct research on processes of cultural globalization (Gupta and Ferguson 1997). The most obvious drawback of culture areas is that, in reality, cultural variation tends to be continuous rather than abrupt. Cultural groups near boundary thus become 'intermediate'. Also, many traits cut across culture area boundaries: cultural variation is complex and not easily reduced to geographical patterns. Despite these problems, the culture area concept is extremely useful as a device for studying ethnographic diversity that it may be taken into account for investigation of general patterns.

Box 1.1 Topic: Unexplained Mysteries

Great ancient cities based on older civilizations have always been built in earthquake zones, where great ideas, different cultures and even the Earth's plates joined together. On a map of the eastern hemisphere, scientists have studied the locations of the Earth's plates and the founding of thirteen ancient cities. They have discovered that eleven of the thirteen great ancient cities were built within 120 miles of the edge of the Eurasian plate, which is too many and too close to be just a coincidence. The eleven cities include Rome, Corinth, Mycenae, Jerusalem and Hastinapura in India. The other two cities were Memphis in Egypt, and Zhengzhou in China. The great plates of the Earth frequently crash into each other, which often results in active volcanoes, earthquakes and floods. Some of these natural disasters seem to stop cultural development, while others seem to help. The reason why great ancient cities tended to grow up near the edges of the Earth's plates remains unclear to scientists.

Eric R. Force, a geologist from the University of Arizona, points out one interesting possibility. Frequent earthquakes, volcanoes, floods or other natural disasters destroy the old cities that are the homes of old cultures and customs, making it possible for the birth of new cultures and customs. Force also finds that the ancient cities based on older civilizations were built closer to edges of the Earth's plates than self-developing societies.

Read the passage and choose the best answer for each question.

1. On a map of the eastern hemisphere, scientists find that (A) all thirteen great ancient cities were built very close to the edge of the Eurasian plate; (B) eleven of the thirteen great ancient cities collapsed; (C) all thirteen great ancient cities were built very close to each other; (D) eleven of the thirteen great ancient cities were built very close to the edge of the Eurasian plate.
2. The crashing of the Earth's plates (A) either helps or stops cultural development; (B) helps human beings to learn more about the world; (C) stops human beings from improving their culture; (D) helps human beings to develop new culture.
3. Cities that lay closer to the edges of the Earth's plates (A) usually developed by themselves; (B) were more likely to give birth to new cultures; (C) developed from other cultures; (D) lasted longer than those further from the edges of the Earth's plates.
4. Which of the following is the best title for the passage? (A) Why Were Great Cities Built in Earthquake Zones? (B) Why Did Great Cultures and Customs Die? (C) What Are the Results of the Crashing of the Earth's Plates? (D) What Are the Advantages of Earthquakes?

(Answers: 1-D, 2-A, 3-B, and 4-A)
Source China Educational Society (2009).

References

Aono T (1979) New geography (B) (in Japanese). Nigong Shiyoten, Tokyo

Bacon E (1946) A preliminary attempt to determine the culture areas of Asia. Southwest J Anthropol 2:117–132

Bagby P (1958) Culture and history: prolegomena to the comparative study of civilizations. Longmans, Green, London

Braudel F (1994) History of civilizations. Allen Lane-Penguin Press, New York

Bros P (2005) The case for the flood. In: Kenyon JD (ed) Forbidden history, Rochester. Bear & Company, Vermont

Brown N (2005) Friedrich Ratzel, Clark Wissler, and Carl Sauer: Culture area research and mapping. Available. www.csiss.org/classics/content/15. Accessed 12 Nov 2008

Buzan B (1991) New patterns of global security in the twenty-first century. Int Affairs 67:441–449

China Educational Society (2009) Unexplained mysteries (section B). English learners' lighthouse (yingyu xuexi fudao bao), No. 50 (8 June) (an English-Chinese version). Available. www.ell.cn/pSmallClass.asp?typeid=32&BigClassID=61&SmallClassID=102. Accessed 10 Aug 2009

Darwin C (1859) The origin of species by means of natural selection, 1st edn. John Murray, London

Driver H (1962) The contribution of A. L. Kroeber to culture area theory and practice. Indians University publications in anthropology and linguistics, no. 18, Waverly Press, Baltimore

Elmandjra M (1994) Cultural diversity: key to survival in the future. Paper presented to the First Mexican Congress on future studies, Mexico City, Sept 1994
Farrand L (1904) Basis of American history, 1500–1900. Ungar, New York
Force ER (2008) Tectonic environments of Ancient civilizations in the Eastern Hemisphere. Geoarchaeol Int J 23(5):644–653
Galtung J (1992) The emerging conflict formations. In: Tehranian K, Tehranian M (eds) Restructuring for world peace: on the threshold of the twenty-first century. Cresskill: Hampton Press, pp 20–39
Gelles PH (2000) Water and power in Highland Peru: the cultural politics of irrigation and development. Rutgers University Press, Fredericksburg
Gilpin R (1993) The cycle of great powers: has it finally been broken?. Princeton University, Princeton
Gupta A, Ferguson J (1997) Culture, power, place: explorations in critical anthropology. Duke University Press, Durham
Guo R (2009) On the birth of ancient civilizations—comments on a paper by Eric R Force. Geoarchaeol Int J 24(6):846–848
Holms W (1903) Classification and arrangement of the exhibits of an Anthropological Museum. Government Printing Office, Washington, DC
Huntington SP (1996) The clash of civilization and the remaking of world order. Simon & Schuster, New York
International Encyclopedia of the Social Sciences (1972) Sills DL (ed) vol. 3, The Macmillan Company and The Free Press, New York, Collier-Macmillan Publishers, London
Keim M (2007) The public health consequences of disasters. Atlanta: Centers for Disease Control and Prevention (CDC). Available. www.dhss.mo.gov/BT_Response/presentations/PublicHealthAndDisasters-Keim.ppt. Accessed 10 Aug 2007
Kendall HM (1976) Introduction to cultural geography. Arnold, London
Kroeber AL (1939) Cultural and natural areas of native North America. University of California Press, Berkeley
Kroeber AL (1947) Culture groupings in Asia. Southwest J Anthropol 3:322–330
Lind M (1990) American as an ordinary country. Am Enterp 1:19–23
Lind WS (1992) North-South relation: returning to a world of cultures in conflict. Curr World Lead 35:1075–1080
Lind WS (1994) Defending Western culture. Foreign Policy 84:40–50
Malakoff D (2008) Did rumbling give rise to Rome? ScienceNOW Daily News, 22 Aug Available. http://sciencenow.sciencemag.org/cgi/content/full/2008/822/3. Accessed 1 Jan 2009
McNeil WH (1963) The rise of the West: a history of the human community. University of Chicago Press, Chicago
Melko M (1969) The nature of civilizations. Porter Sargent, Boston
Naroll RS (1950) A draft map of the culture areas of Asia. Southwest J Anthropol 6:183–187
Patai R (1951) Nomadism: Middle Eastern and Central Asian. Southwest J Anthropol 7:401–414
Puchala DJ (1994) The history of the future of international relations. Ethics Int Aff 8:177–202
Quigley C (1979) The evolution of civilizations: an introduction to historical analysis, 2nd edn. Liberty Press, Indianapolis
Reebs S (2008) Creative destruction—ancient civilizations rose near tectonic boundaries. Natural history magazine, December 2008–January 2009. Available. www.naturalhistorymag.com/samplings/11343/creative-destruction. Accessed 20 Oct 2009
Rostovanyi Z (1993) Clash of civilizations and cultures: Unity or disunity of world order. Unpublished paper, March
Sapper K (1968) The Verapaz in the sixteenth and seventeenth centuries: a contribution to the historical geography and ethnography of Northeastern Guatemala. Occasional papers of the Institute of Archaeology, UCLA, Los Angeles, No. 13
Scarborough VL (2003) The flow of power: ancient water systems and landscapes. SAR Press, Santa Fe

ScienceNOW Staff (2008) The top 10 ScienceNOWs of 2008. ScienceNOW Daily News, 24 Dec 2008

Sinclair K (1987) The yellow river: a 5000 year journey through China. Child & Associates Publishing, Chatswood, Sydney, Australia

Spengler O (1928) Decline of the West. A. A. Knopf, New York

Stewart D Jr (2008) Evidence of the global genesis flood. Available. www.scripturehistory.com/globalflood.php. Accessed 22 Oct 2008

The Economist (1994) The new world order: back to the future. Oxford University Press, London, pp 21–23

Toynbee A (1961) A study of history. Oxford University Press, London

Vlahos M (1991) Culture and foreign policy. Foreign Policy 82:59–78

Wissler C (1917) The American Indian: an introduction to the anthropology of the New World, 3rd edn. Smith, Gloucester

Wittfogel KA (1957) Oriental despotism: A comparative study of total power. Yale University Press, New Haven, Conn

Worsher D (1985) Rivers of empire: water, aridity, and growth of the American West. Pantheon Books, New York

Chapter 2
After Cultures Meet

Abstract No culture is isolated from other cultures. Nor is any culture changeless, invariant or static. All cultures are in a state of constant flux, driven by both internal and external forces. All of these are the inherent dynamics of the multiculturally based world per se. In this chapter, beginning with the question 'why Mesopotamia had the oldest civilization in the world', the spatial interaction of ancient civilizations is assessed; and four non-linear patterns of intercultural dynamics are presented. Our empirical analyses of the four major ancient civilizations (the Mesopotamian, the Egyptian, the Indus, and the Chinese) focus on intercultural influences as well as how they have shaped the spatial dynamics of the world as a whole.

Keywords Ancient civilization · Adjacency · Intercultural dynamics · Mesopotamia · Spatial interaction

2.1 Focus on Mesopotamia

In Chap. 1, we have discussed the natural and geographical factors contributing to the birth of ancient civilizations. Some empirical evidence has also explained to some extent why existing cultures and culture areas are conflicting and complementary. Till now, many issues relating to the origin of and evolution of ancient civilizations are still puzzling both anthropologists and human geographers. They include such questions as: Why Mesopotamia has the oldest civilization in the world? Why is the Chinese civilization younger than the other three ancient civilizations (i.e., ancient Egyptian, the ancient Indus and the Mesopotamian)? Why have some ancient civilizations eventually become extinct while others not? What are the driving forces for the human civilizations to grow, to expand and to decline eventually? Before dealing with these issues, let us first look at the spatial mechanism of cultural formation in Mesopotamia.

R. Guo, *Introduction to Intercultural Economics*, SpringerBriefs in Economics,
DOI: 10.1007/978-3-642-29276-7_2, © The Author(s) 2012

The Euphrates and the Tigris run parallel to each other.[1] The land between the Euphrates and the Tigris is known as Mesopotamia, which means "between the rivers" in Greek. The Tigris and the Euphrates provided much of the water that supported the development of ancient Mesopotamian culture. The Euphrates is the longest river of western Asia. More than two-thirds of the entire course of the river is navigable for boats. The Euphrates has its springs in the highlands of Eastern Turkey and its mouth at the Persian Gulf. It is formed in Turkey by two major tributaries—the Murat and the Karasu Rivers—both of them rise from the Armenian mountains. These two streams join together near the city of Elazig, and the Euphrates follows a southeastern route to enter Syria at Karakamis point. After entering Syria, the Euphrates continues its southeastern course and is joined by two more tributaries, the Khabur and the Balikh. Both of these tributaries have their sources in Turkey and they are the last bodies of water that contribute to the river. After entering Iraq, the river reaches the city of Hit. The Euphrates joins in southeastern Iraq to form the Shatt al Arab, which empties into the Persian Gulf.

The Tigris, like the Euphrates, rises from the Armenian mountains. It has two principal sources, Lake Hazer and Lake Van, both in Anatolia in Eastern Turkey. The Tigris' two streams joins at Til in Turkey. Along its middle and lower courses, the Tigris receives no fewer than five important tributaries of the Zakko or eastern Tigris, the Greater Zab (Zab Ala), the Lesser Zab (Zab Asfal), the Adhem, and the Diyaleh. The city of Baghdad is located on the conjunction of the Tigris and Diyala rivers and navigation is possible from Baghdad downstream. The Tigris follows a southeastern route in Turkey to the city of Cizre, where it forms a section of the boundary between Turkey and Syria before entering Iraq. In Iraq the Tigris meets its tributaries: the Greater Zap, the Lesser Zap, the Adhaim, and the Diyala. It then joins the Euphrates in Qurna and continues its journey as the Shatt al-Arab to the Persian Gulf. Along its course, the Tigris passes through some of the major cities of Iraq, like Mosul, Tikrit, Samarra, and the capital Baghdad.

Mesopotamia has remained as the center of many different civilizations and given natural resources to millions of inhabitants living there. Both the Tigris and the Euphrates have provided much of the water that supported the development of the ancient Mesopotamian culture. The Tigris-Euphrates valley was the birthplace of the ancient civilizations of Assyria, Babylonia and Sumer. In northern Iraq the Euphrates forms the western boundary of the area known as Al Jazirah. To the southeast the alluvial lands between the two rivers was the site of the glorious Babylonian civilizations of ancient times. According to the historical data yielded by archaeological excavations on the banks of the Tigris and the Euphrates, irrigation made it possible for the locals to develop agriculture within the Euphrates-Tigris

[1] Historically, the Euphrates derives its name from the Sumarian Buranun, which became Purattum in Akadian, Ufrat in old Persian, Euphrates in Greek and Latin, Furat in Arabic, and Firat in Turkish. The name for the Tigris comes from the Sumerian Idigna, which became Idiglat in Akkadian, Tigra in old Persian, and Tigris to Herodotus (c. 450 BC) and those after him. Modern Turks refer to it as the Dicle, which is also the Arabic name. Cited from Kolars and Mitchell (1991, pp. 4 and 8).

valley (Kolars and Mitchell 1991). This resulted in the development of great ancient civilizations within the Tigris-Euphrates valley, where water played an important starting role. The Euphrates has been an important river up through history, and the Tigris too contributed greatly to the birth of ancient civilizations.

The major contribution of the Tigris and the Euphrates to the civilizations was their suitability to irrigation, and as a result the earliest farmlands were developed within the Tigris-Euphrates valley. To control these floods, the Iraqis divert water from the Tigris to the Euphrates, where the Euphrates has less alleviation than the Tigris. At Samarra a barrage is constructed, in order to improve the control of the floods that can occur between March and May, when snow melts in the mountains. This barrage also was constructed to provide better irrigation. The Euphrates and the Tigris were turbulent and many sections of them were unsuitable for traffic. At times, floodwaters would destroy large areas. Because of the irregularities of the tributaries' flows, the Tigris is widely known for its infamous floods. Furthermore, during the ancient times the land between the Euphrates and the Tigris had remained as the center of human activities that were seriously influenced by the two parallel rivers via even more complicated ways than any other parts of the world. Consequently, the Mesopotamian people were required to form a more centralized rule and to invent more technical wisdoms in order to give a simultaneous control over the floods occurring at *both* rivers than other peoples in the rest of the world.[2] The final result is that Mesopotamia—an area with the most complicated river systems—gave birth to an oldest civilization in the world.

2.2 Spatial Adjacency and Culture

The development of any culture consists of inventing new things and forgetting old ones (Bauman 1999, p. 73). During prehistoric period human civilization did not exist or, at least, only appeared as that in a preliminary stage. Thus, some cultural elements—language and religion—were at only a primitive level; and the intercultural differences were very small. An interesting fact suggests that certain languages might be related in that they have evolved from a common ancestral language (Sapir 1949). As a result intercultural difference increased. Witness to this are, for example, the newly born forms of Christianity in the Western World (see Fig. 2.1). On the other and, there has been a sign of interculturalization during the civilizational era. In the past thousands of years, technological progress, division of social labor, intercultural trade, immigration as well as wars, have speeded up cultural diffusion throughout the world. Witness to this is the widespread of many ethnic (such as Anglo-Saxon, and Han-Chinese), linguistic (such as Chinese, English, French, Portuguese, Russian, and Spanish) and religious (such as Buddhism, Christianity,

[2] One may find evidence to support the close relationship between river flood and the birth of ancient civilizations from Tables 1.1 and 1.2 of Chap. 1.

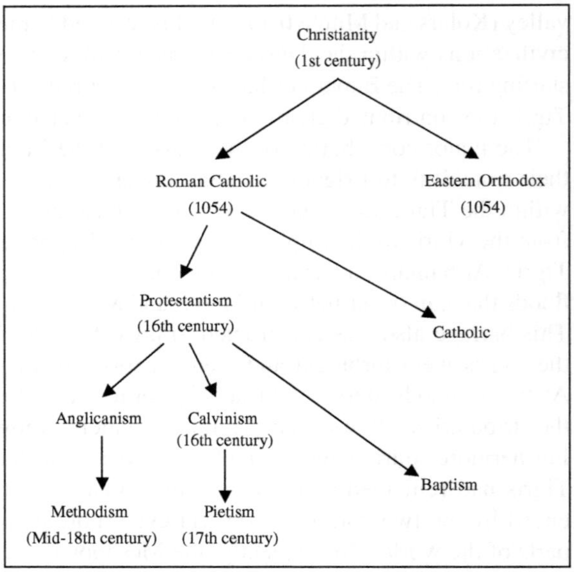

Fig. 2.1 Christianity and its major sects

Confucianism, and Islam) groups that had only one or two geographical origins at the early times.[3]

With close proximity to Mesopotamia, there had been two other ancient civilizations in today's Egypt and India. The Egyptians have had a very different relationship with the Nile. For thousands of years, they referred to its annual flooding as the "Gift of the Nile." Each summer, like clockwork, the river would take possession of a strip of land on either side of its bank. When the water receded, a very thin, evenly spread layer of black mud was left behind. Farmers would immediately plant their crops—never needing fertilizers because the flood soil itself was so rich. This narrow strip along the Nile, together with the delta at the river's northern mouth, is the only farmland Egypt has. Egypt's farmland is less than 30 thousand square kilometers (only 3% of the country's total land area), which is obviously far less than India's and China's. Furthermore, surrounded by the Mediterranean sea in the north, the Libyan desert (As Sahra al Libiyah) in the west, the Arabian desert in the east, and the Nubian desert in the south, Egypt has no extra hinterland in the African continent. The limited sizes of land and of, naturally, the population might be a reason for the ancient Egyptian civilization to decline and, after being conquered by outside forces, to become extinct eventually.[4]

India's extraordinary history is intimately tied to its geography. A meeting ground between the East and the West, India has always been an invader's paradise, while at the same time its natural isolation and the magnetic pull of its religions

[3] See Appendix A for the current status of the ethnic, linguistic and religious characteristics of the world.

[4] For a detailed analysis of the spatial optimality of cultures, see Guo (2009, pp. 41–76).

allowed it to adapt to and absorb many of the peoples who penetrated its mountain passes. Around 5,000 years ago, an important civilization developed on the Indus floodplain. From about 2,600 to 1,700 BC a vast number of settlements were built on the banks of the Indus and the surrounding areas. Indus civilization remnants have been discovered from as far south as Mumbai in India, and as far north as the Himalayas and northern Afghanistan. The westernmost sites are on the coast of the Arabian sea in Baluchistan, Pakistan, right next to the Iranian border. Archaeological work confirms that there has been another large river (i.e., the Saraswati-Ghaggar-Hakra river) in the east of and parallel to the Indus in the third and fourth millennium BC. In the Indus and Ghaggar-Hakra river valleys, in what is today Pakistan and western India, it developed around 2,500 BC into the Harappa or Indus valley civilization on the Indian subcontinent.[5] The people of the Indus valley civilization achieved great mastery in measuring length, mass, and time. Engineers already followed the decimal division of measurement. In the coastal city of Harappa, remarkable docks were built after studying the effects of tides, waves, and currents (Coppa et al. 2006). Although it is still a myth that the ancient Indus civilization declined suddenly around 1700 BC, the major causes may include the Aryan invasion and the drying up of the ancient Saraswati-Ghaggar-Hakra river.

The valley of the Yellow river is the cradle of Chinese civilization. During the past thousands of years, the Yellow river has played a crucial role in China's civilizational development. The management of the Yellow river has cost large amount of physical and human capitals and, consequently, generated various technologies and wisdoms, all of which have become important elements of the Chinese culture. Attempts at controlling the Yellow river began, according to existing historical records, as early as the twenty-second century BC. A great engineer named Yu was appointed to take preventive measures after a disastrous flood, who came up with the idea of dredging the river to encouraging the water to flow in its proper channel. Yu later was made the emperor of China's first dynasty, the Xia, for his contribution to the control of terrible flooding of the Yellow river. The Yellow river had bore the test of almost all kinds of upheavals and difficulties, and finally created the continuous Chinese civilization (see the latter part of Sect. 1.1 of Chap. 1 for more detailed evidence). And again, to some extent, Yellow river also is the symbol of the spirit of the Chinese people: grittiness, industriousness and assiduity.

Without considering geographical factor, it could be very difficult to understand the patterns of both global and regional development. For instance, bilateral trade flows across the US-Canadian border, between France, Italy, UK, Germany and the Netherlands, and along the western coast of the Pacific Ocean (including, *inter alia*, South Korea, Taiwan, Hong Kong and the mainland of China) have risen a great deal more quickly than those between remote and isolated economies. Besides distance, another proxy of geographical factor exerting influences on international trade is adjacency. For example, bilateral trade between France and

[5] This phase is contemporary to the Early to Middle Bronze Age, to Mesopotamian Ur III, prepalatial Minoan Cretem, and the First Intermediate Egyptian Period.

the United Kingdom will be due to their proximity, but trade between France and Germany will be further boosted by their common border. For example, in Frankel et al. (1997, p. 66) estimated result, the coefficients on 'adjacency' range between 0.5 and 0.7. Because trade is specified in natural logarithmic form in their model, the way to interpret the coefficients on adjacency is to take the exponent: that is to say, two countries that share a common border will, *ceteris paribus*, increase their trade by about 65–101 % compared with two otherwise countries.[6]

Now let us examine the role that geographical adjacency has played in the interactions and dynamics of the early civilizations in the eastern hemisphere. Due to their geographical proximity to Mesopotamia, the Nile and the Indus valleys have been able to receive direct cultural influences from Mesopotamia, and vice versa. This might be the primary reason for the Nile and the Indus valleys (and also, of course, the Mesopotamia) to have an earlier civilization than the Yellow river valley. The major excavations which were first carried out by the joint Pakistani American Harappa Archaeological Research Project (HARP) in 1986, have shown that the ancient Indus civilization might have gradually spread from west to east. This might have been the result of intercultural trade with Mesopotamia—the first major ancient civilization in the world. Ancient Mesopotamian texts speak of trading with at least two seafaring civilizations—Magan and Meluhha—in the neighborhood of South Asia in the third millennium BC. This trade was conducted with real financial sophistication in amounts that could involve tones of copper. The Mesopotamians speak of Meluhha as a land of exotic commodities. A wide variety of objects produced in the Indus valley have been found at sites in Mesopotamia.[7]

During ancient times, given the unavailability of transportation via air or at sea, Chinese civilization was geographically isolated from the other, earlier civilizations in Asia. The Himalayas between China and India and the Pamirs in central Asia had been the major geographical obstacles for China to receive cultural influences from the Indus and the Mesopotamian civilizations during the pre-modern times. For example, in the Tang dynasty (AD 618–907) a Chinese Buddhist pilgrim, named Xuanzang (AD 602–664), conducted a 16-year visit to India in AD 629, bringing back 657 copies of Sanskrit manuscripts to China. The 12-volumne monograph entitled *Datang Xiyu Ji* (the great Tang record of a journey to the West), written by Xuanzang's disciples, tells how the trip from China to India was full with innumerable hardships. By contrast, the Mesopotamian, the Egyptian and the Indus civilizations could easily exert influences on and, at the same time, receive influences from each other. The final result may be that the ancient Chinese civilization is much younger than the other three ancient civilizations (see Table 2.1 for a comparison of these ancient civilizations).

---

[6] See Chap. 3 for a detailed quantitative analysis of geographical influences on international trade.

[7] Cited from an article available at www.harappa.com/har/indus-saraswati.html. Accessed 7 April 2009.

Table 2.1 A brief comparison of the world's four ancient civilizations

	Ancient Egyptian	Mesopotamian	Ancient indus[a]	Chinese
Appearance of written language	3100 BC (hieroglyphic writing)	3300 BC (pictographic writing)	1500 BC (Vedic—an early form of Sanskrit)	1384 BC (*jiaguwen*—characters found on oracle bones)
Creation of religion or law with written texts	2350 BC (inscription in the burial chamber)	1755 BC[b] (Hammurabi code)	1500 BC (Brahmanism)	1044 BC (*Zhouli*—rites of the Zhou dynasty)
Invention of calendar or time measurement	3000 BC	3000 BC	2500 BC	1766 BC
Date of birth of state(s)	3100 BC (1st dynasty)	3500 BC (six city-states)	750 BC (16 kingdoms or *mahajanapadas*)	1988 BC (Xia dynasty)

[a] Since most ancient civilizations developed within the Harappa or Indus valleys had become extinct before 1700 BC, some figures shown in this column may not be accurate

[b] Hammurabi created the first code of laws (using the Babylonian language) in the world

2.3 Patterns of Intercultural Dynamics

A glance at the process of the world's civilizational evolutions during the past thousands of years simply reveals that no civilizations (or countries) have been economic and technological leaders forever. There are various historical cases in which a culture was invaded and eventually replaced by another culture. But it is more common to think of historical episodes in which a gradual cumulative process of divergence does seem to have been at work; one need only think of India's industrial and commercial leadership in the last centuries before the Christ, or China's widening technological leadership in the first and the first half of the second millenniums after the Christ. For example, paper was introduced in China in the second century AD, came to Japan in the seventh century, and was diffused westward to Central Asia in the eighth century, North Africa in the tenth, Spain in the twelfth and northern Europe in the thirteenth. Printing was invented in China in the eighth century AD and movable type in the eleventh century, but this technology only reached Europe in the fifteenth century. Another Chinese invention, gunpowder, made in the ninth century, disseminated to the Arabs after a few 100 years and eventually reached Europe in the fourteenth century (Braudel 1981, p. 14).

Since the seventeenth or eighteenth century, the Western civilization has been far more developed than the rest of the world. As mentioned in Weber (1904, pp. 1–2), only in the West did modern science exist at a stage of development which we reorganize today as valid. Empirical knowledge, reflection on problems of the cosmos and life, philosophical and theological wisdom of the most profound sort, are not confined to it, though in the case of the last the full development of a systematic theology must be credited to Christianity under the influence of Hellenism, since there were only fragments in Islam and in a few of Indian sects. Although the knowledge and observation of great refinement have existed in all ancient civilizations, they lack scientific foundations. For example, the Indian geometry had no rational proofs; that was another product of the Greek intellect, also the creator of mechanics and physics. The ancient Indian and Chinese natural sciences, though well developed in observation, lacked the method of experiment, which was, apart from beginning in antiquity, essentially a product of the Renaissance, as was modern laboratory. Hence medicine in China and India, though highly developed in empirical technique, lacked a biological and particularly a biochemical foundation.

Economists have characterized the mechanism of international competition in securing technological leadership by a leapfrogging process.[8] To this end, the international patterns of incremental technological change are explained (see, for example, Brezis et al. 1993). Theoretical and empirical analyses have concluded that, given their extensive experience with older technologies, leading nations may have no incentive to adopt new ideas; lagging nations, however, have less experience with the old technologies, may grasp the opportunity to break into the

[8] Leapfrog is a game in which one player kneels or bends over while the next in line leaps over him or her.

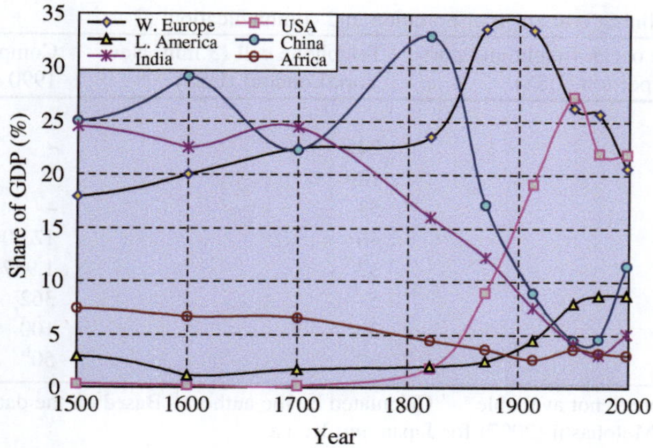

Fig. 2.2 A dynamic view of the world economy, AD 1500—2000 *Source* Created by the author based on Maddison (2001)

market (see, for example, Jovanovic and Nyakro 1994; and Barro and Sala-i-Martin 1995, Chap. 8). If the new techniques eventually prove to be more productive than the old techniques, there is a reversal of leadership. While individual countries have established long periods of economic and technological leadership, such periods of dominance are not forever. The early modern preeminence of the Dutch was ended by the rise of England; and England's preeminence by the rise of Germany and America. If the current world growth pattern (see Fig. 2.2) persists for two or more decades, we may be seeing the U.S. overtaken by China or India in the twenty-first century.

Technology has been the most fundamental element in promoting intercultural influences. In pre-modern times the spread of ideas and technology could take centuries. Intercontinent journeys, which now only need a few hours via air, would have taken several months before the twentieth century. Technological advances in communication have made it possible to know in an instant what is happening in a household or factory or on a stock market half a world away. The growing importance of services and information in the world economy means that an increasing proportion of economic value is weightless—that is, it can be transmitted over fiber-optic cable rather than transported in a container ship. At the same time improvements in transportation networks and technology are reducing the costs of shipping goods by water, ground and air and improvements in information technology have made it easier to raise productivity, as well as to increase intercultural specialization of labor (see Table 2.2). More important are the improvements in information technology (IT) that have made it easier to manage the new interconnections worldwide via Internet, the fast-growing tool of communication. The Internet has provided a new means of commerce, with clear speed and cost advantages.

Table 2.2 Declining costs of transportation and communication

Year	Average ocean freight and port charges per ton (US$)	Telephone call (3 min, New York/London) (US$)	Computers (index, 1990 = 100)
1920	95	–	–
1930	60	245	–
1940	63	189	–
1950	34	53	–
1960	27	46	12,500
1970	27	32	1,947
1980	24	5	362
1990	29	3	100
2000[a]	–	<1	50[b]

Notes "–" denotes "not available". [a] Calculated by the author. [b] Based on the data estimated by Kanamori and Motohashi (2007) for Japan and Korea
Source IMF (1997), except those that are noted otherwise

When a new technology becomes available, however, it may not initially seem much better than the old one—and to a nation that has established a commanding lead in the old technology, it may well seem worse. Thus eighteenth century Holland, with its established lead in shipping, banking and trading, was not attracted by the prospects of cotton spinning; it was the somewhat poorer English who moved into the new area and exploited its eventually far greater potential (Brezis et al. 1993, p. 1212). Such a failure to take advantage of new technologies may seem in retrospect like short-sightedness. In fact, however, it may have been a fully rational decision from the point of view of individual entrepreneurs. A country with an established lead will be a high wage nation; new technologies or industries that are initially less productive than the old one are therefore not profitable. It is only a lagging nation, where the old technology is less well developed and hence wages are lower, that the new, relatively untried techniques seem attractive. Such economic and technological 'leapfrogging' could be essentially random: lagging countries may simply get luck, leading countries get unlucky. And, indeed, the divergent patterns could be explained, at least partially, by what has been noted in Landes (1966, p. 563): "Prosperity and success are their own worst enemies".[9]

Cultural diffusion is generally taken to mean the spread of a culture from one area or ethnic group to another area or ethnic group. Diffusion has always had a catalytic function in cultural development, as the comparatively rapid growth of human culture as a whole has risen from the ability of all societies to borrow

[9] Brezis et al. (1993, p. 1219) give a number of conditions under which there will be a leapfrogging process: (i) The difference in wage costs between the leading nation and potential challengers must be large. (ii) The new technology must, when viewed by experienced producers, appear initially unproductive compared with the old one. (iii) Experience in the old technology must not be too useful in the new technology. (iv) The new technology must ultimately offer the possibility of substantial productivity improvement over the old.

elements from other cultures and to incorporate them into their own. Moreover, the necessity of integrating newly acquired elements into one's cultural heritage both creates new problems (such as the so called 'clash of civilizations' as mentioned in Huntington's (1993) article) and engenders new ideas. It was the opportunity for relatively rapid interchange of inventions and ideas between different cultures that either made possible the birth of newer civilizations or promoted the old civilizations to advance further.

Indeed, the clash of civilizations is not a welcoming event in contemporary society. And it did lead to both emotional and physical damages to human beings, especially at the first stage of the clash. However, the history of civilizations has told that the clash of civilizations is inevitable in many cases and it might yield positive effects on the progressive evolution of civilizations in the long-run, if not the short-run. One example witness to the inter-civilizational dynamics may be found in the Eastern Hemisphere where the Mesopotamian, the ancient Egyptian and the ancient Indus civilizations were exerting influences on and benefiting from each other. It is argued that it probably was the significance of the intercultural influences that made the birth of these three civilizations much earlier than that of the ancient Chinese civilization (as discussed in Sect. 2.2 of Chap. 2).

In order to clarify the dynamic patterns of intercultural influences, let us consider a simplified case in which the so-called 'clash' occurs between a 'leading' culture and a 'lagging' culture. Although the leading culture has a higher average level in technological progress than the lagging one, the lagging culture also has some technological advantages over the leading one. Thus, we suppose that each culture will develop (grow) via a linear pattern (as shown by the dot lines in Fig. 2.3). If the two cultures meet in a specific space, then there will be different, non-linear development patterns for both the leading and the lagging cultures. In the following, we define four types of patterns for these two cultures' developments over time:

Pattern 1. If the lagging culture invades the leading culture but fails eventually, the development of the leading culture follows the pattern shown in Fig. 2.3a.

Pattern 2. If the leading culture invades the lagging culture but fails eventually, the development of the lagging culture follows the pattern shown in Fig. 2.3b.

Pattern 3. If the lagging culture invades the leading culture and wins eventually, the development of the leading culture follows the pattern shown in Fig. 2.3c.

Pattern 4. If the leading culture invades the lagging culture and wins eventually, the development of the lagging culture follows the pattern shown in Fig. 2.3d.

2.4 Intercultural Influences

No culture is not influenced by, and does not influence, other cultures. Nor is any culture changeless, invariant or static. All cultures are in a state of constant flux, driven by both internal and external forces. In Chap. 1, we have examined the various internal factors contributing to the birth of and the evolution of ancient

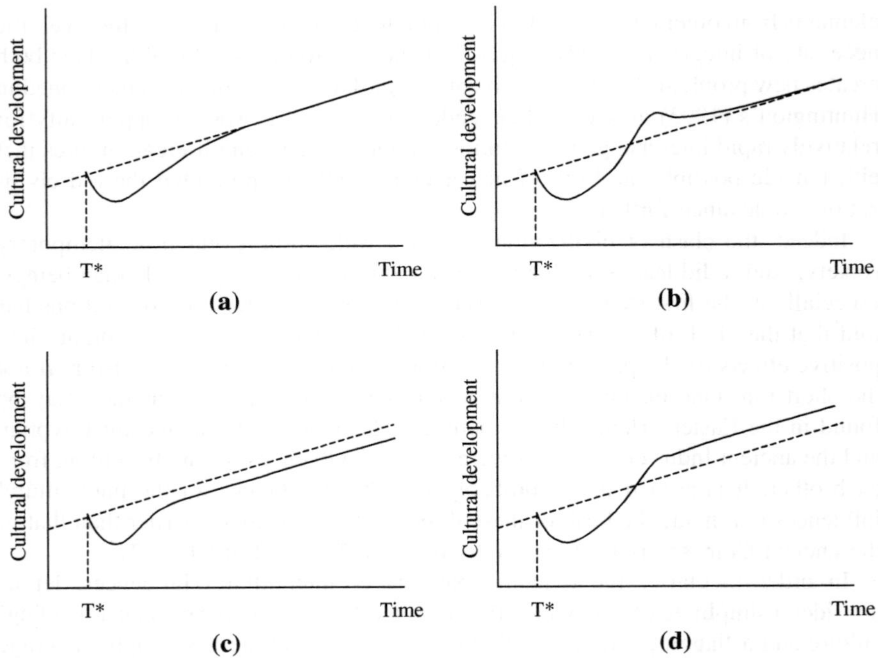

Fig. 2.3 Patterns of cultural development under different external conditions. *Notes* (1) T* denotes the date at which a foreign culture invades; (2) dot lines denote the normal pattern of cultural development

civilizations. In fact, when trying to answer such question as why there were no great ancient civilizations in America, we should also pay attention to other factors. In some circumstances, external factors (such as intercultural contacts and exchanges) are also very importantly influencing culture change. For example, internal factor played an important role in the cultural development of North America before the fifteenth century, while external factor played an important role after the New World was found in 1492. Of course, we still need more detailed evidence in order to reach the conclusion that America's geographical isolation could have resulted in the declining of its early civilizations. However, a comparison of the North American Prairie nomads and the Eurasian Steppe nomads—which are thought to be blood relatives—simply suggests that external influence should matter to the evolution of civilizations (see Box 2.1).

Most anthropologists would agree in that the earliest human societies must have been small and simple in social organization, and poor in technological equipment. As a result cultures must have been highly diversified. Since these characteristics contrast greatly with modern industrial societies, we must think that the world has experienced some forms of integration of adjacent cultures throughout the world. There are six forms of cultural integration. The first type of cultural integration is called 'configurational or thematic integration'. It refers to an identity of meaning

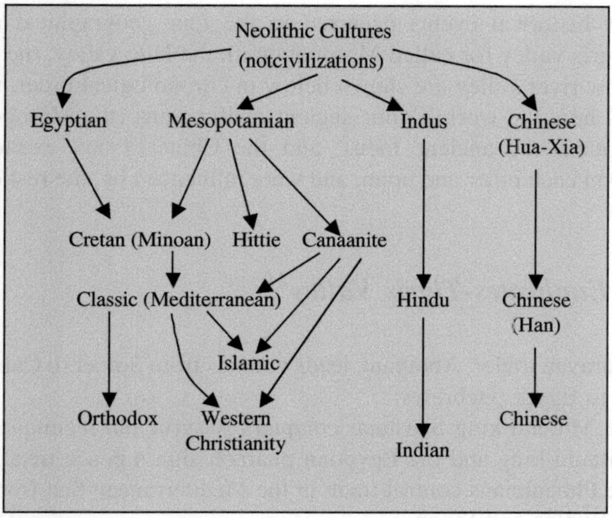

Fig. 2.4 The dynamic relations among major civilizations of the world

within a diversity of cultural items: their conformity to a common pattern, their embodiment of a common theme. Connective integration is the second type of cultural integration that concerns the extent to which the diverse parts of culture are directly connected with one another. A third dimension of integration (or logical integration) concerns the extent to which cultural items tend to contradict one another. This perspective defines integration not as identity or as interlocking diversity but in terms of logical consistency—a criterion that primarily affects existential beliefs and systems of norms. The fourth form is known as the adaptive or functional integration. A fifth type of integration (stylistic integration) is that which emerges from the mutual adaptation of parts of experience felt so intensively that their contrasts and organization produce an emotionally gratifying whole. Its locus is those characteristic modes of behavior and manners of expression we term styles. Finally, the sixth form of cultural integration is called regulative integration.[10]

A brief glance at the evolutions of human civilizations reveals that the interaction of civilizations has existed frequently in many places of the world. The world's civilizations have evolved through different phases, since they first emerged 5,000 years ago. Some regions witnessed two or three generations of affiliated cultures, with the demise of one culture and interregnum followed by the rise of another successor generation. A simplified chart of the dynamic relations among the major ancient civilizations and their successors is shown in Fig. 2.4.

[10] Cited from Levine (1972, pp. 375–8).

The major historical events occurred in the four geographical areas of the Euphrates-Tigris valley (or called Mesopotamia), the Nile valley, the Indus valley and the Yellow river valley are shown below in chronological order, respectively. They can tell how the world's four ancient civilizations (the Mesopotamian, the ancient Egyptian, the ancient Indus, and the Chinese) had exerted profound influences upon each other and upon, and were influenced by, the rest of the world.

2.4.1 The Euphrates-Tigris Valley[11]

1500 BC: a caravan trader, Abraham, leads nomads from Sumer to Canaan and then on to Egypt (Hebrews)
1400 BC: the Mitanni king Saustatar conquers Assyria and reconquers Syria; the Mitanni king and the Egyptian pharaoh sign a peace treaty
1000 BC: the Phoenicians control trade in the Mediterranean Sea from their bases in Byblos and Sidon
671 BC: the Assyrians capture the Egyptian capital of Memphis
664 BC: the Assyrians conquers Thebes
653 BC: the Scythians invade the Median empire (northeast Persia); Assyria destroys the Elamite kingdom
612 BC: the Babylonians split the Assyrian empire (Mesopotamia to Babylon and Elam to Media) while Egypt recovers control of Palestine and Syria
605 BC: the Babylonians conquer Carchemish and defeat the Egyptian army
525 BC: Cambyses of Persia conquers Egypt
521 BC: Persia empire expands beyond the Indus River
514 BC: the Persians invade Scythia
490 BC: Persia attacks mainland Greece
480 BC: the Greeks expels the Persians from Europe
334 BC: Alexander defeats the Persian army at the Dardanelles
333 BC: Alexander invades the Persian empire from Syria to Palestine
331 BC: Alexander the Great conquers Persia and destroys Persepolis
282 BC: Seleucus conquers Asia Minor
261 BC: Antiochus II (Seleucid) fights the Egyptians
250 BC: the Parni invade the satrapy of Parthia (northern Iran) and found the Parthian empire
225 BC: the Celts in the west and the Sarmatians in the east destroy the Scythian kingdom
198 BC: the Seleucids conquer Palestine and Phoenicia from the Ptolemaics
192 BC: the Seleucids under Antiochus III are defeated by the Romans in Thracia
190 BC: Bactrian king Euthydemus defeats Seleucid king Antiochus III at Magnesia

[1] Based on Toynbee (1961), Zhao (2001) and other sources.

188 BC: Pergamum conquers the Seleucid lands of Lydia, Phrygia, Lycaonia, Pisidia
185 BC: Parthians expand into Seleucid eastern Iran
170 BC: Batrian king Demetrios I expands Bactria to northwestern India
165 BC: the Maccabeans revolt in Palestine and gain independence from the Seleucids
155 BC: Bactrian king Menander invades northwestern India
141 BC: the Parthians conquer Media and Elam from the Seleucids
127 BC: the Parthians are defeated by the Scythians
126 BC: the Parthians conquer Babylonia from the Seleucids
124 BC: the Parthians are defeated again by the Scythians
106 BC: Mithirdates II signs a treaty with China to open the "silk road"
92 BC: Mithridates II signs a peace treaty with Rome
69 BC: Rome invades Tigranes' Armenian kingdom
80 BC: the Scythians (Saka) conquer northwestern India from Bactria
71 BC: Mithridates VI of Pontus is conquered by Rome
64 BC: Syria is conquered by Rome; the Seleucid dynasty ends
63 BC: Pompeus captures Jerusalem and annexes Palestine to Rome
53 BC: the Parthians led by Orodes II defeat the Romans at Carrhae (Syria)
20 BC: Rome and the Parthians fix their boundary along the Euphrates river (Iraq)
50 AD: Christianity emerges from Palestine
116: Roman emperor defeats the Parthian king and conquers Mesopotamia
244: king Shapur I attacks Rome
298: the Sassanids sign a peace treaty with Rome
363: the Sassanids defeat the Roman emperor Julian and recapture Nisibis and Armenia
379: Shapur II conquers Arabia and reaches the border with China
451: Zoroastran Persia (Sassanids) defeats Christian Armenia
484: Zoroastran Persia and Christian Armenia sign a treaty that allows the Armenians to keep their religion
636: the Arabs capture Ctesiphon, the Sassanid empire ends

2.4.2 *The Yellow River Valley*[12]

176 BC: the Huns attack the Han dynasty
121 BC: China defeats the Huns
110 BC: the Silk Road is inaugurated (a treaty between Chinese emperor Wudi and Parthian king Mithridates II)

---

[12] Based on Dai and Gong (2000) and other sources. Note that intercultural influences within the Yellow River valley can date from as early as the twenty-third century BC, but they soon resulted in the integration of a single culture.

48 AD: defeated by the Han dynasty, the Huns dissolves
68 AD: Buddhism is introduced from India to China
372: Buddhism is introduced from China to the kingdom of Koguryo (Korea)
643: Buddhist pilgrim Xuanzang brings sanskrit manuscripts from India to China
650: the Tang dynasty extends the boundaries of China west into Afghanistan, north into Siberia, east into Korea and south into Vietnam, golden age of art and literature (ideal of the universal man, combining the qualities of scholar, poet, painter, statesman)
659: the Tang defeats the western Ashina kaghanate
781: Tibetans occupy Dunhuang
821: Peace treaty between Tibet and China
846: the Kirghiz drive the Uighurs west to the Tarim basin
907: northern invaders terminate the Tang dynasty
1115: the Jurchen/Nuzhen invade from the north and establish the Jin dynasty with capital in Beijing
1125: the Jurchen/Jin force the Song court to move their capital to Hangzhou in the south
1234: Mongols led by Ogodai Khagan conquer northern China and expel the Jurchen
1264: the Mongols invade China and Kublai Khan founds the Yuan dynasty and moves the capital from Karakorum to Khanbaligh (Beijing)
1266: Marco Polo travels from Venice to China
1279: Mongols complete the conquest of entire China and terminate the Song dynasty
1368: China regains independence from the Mongols
1368: the renovation of the Great Wall of China
1389: the Uigurs convert to Islam
1405: Zhenghe (a former Muslim slave) sails west with a fleet of 300 ships, invading Sumatra and Ceylon (Sri Lanka) and eventually reaching the coast of Africa
1550: the renovation of the Great Wall of China is completed
1557: Portugal establishes a trading post in Macau (first European settlement in the Far East)
1583: Jesuit missionary Matteo Ricci arrives in China
1616: Nurhachi unifies the Jurchen (Manchus) and creates the state of Jin (latter named Qing) in northeastern China
1644: the Manchus, led by Dorgon, invade northern China and establish the Qing dynasty
1689: China signs a border treaty with Russia to settle the border between Russian Siberia and Chinese Manchuria
1728: France establishes a trading post in Guangzhou
1729: the emperor issues a decree banning the sale of opium
1757: China invades eastern Turkestan and renames it Xinjiang
1760: all foreign trade is confined to Guangzhou
1840: the Opium war with Britain
1842: China cedes the island of Hong Kong to Britain

1851: the Taiping rebels, with 30 million people killed
1856: China is attacked by British and French forces
1860: British and French forces occupy Beijing; Russia secures north Manchuria
1884: France expands in Indochina after winning a war against China
1895: Japan defeats China and China is forced to cede Taiwan and recognize Japanese sovereignty over Korea
1900: the anti-western Boxer (Yihetuan) rebellion, followed by the invasion of foreign troops including Russia, Britain, France, Japan, USA, etc.
1912: China adopts the Gregorian calendar
1917: China joins World War I on the side of Britain, France, Japan and the USA, the first time ever that Chinese soldiers walk into another continent
1921: Under the the supervision of Soviet agent Borodin, Marxist intellectuals found the communist party of China
1931: the Japanese army invades Manchuria
1933: the Japanese army invades Hebei
1936: Japan invades the northern province of Suiyuan
1937: Japan captures Nanjing (about 300,000 Chinese are killed)
1945: Japan is forced to retreat from China (20 million Chinese dead)
1997: Britain returns Hong Kong to China
1999: Portugal returns Macau to China

2.4.3 *The Nile Valley*[13]

1991 BC: Amenemhet I seizes power (12th dynasty), builds the "Wall of the Prince" in the Sinai to protect Egypt from invasions
1640 BC: An Asian population, the Hyksos, Semitic people from Palestine, seizes power in northern Egypt (the Delta), with capital in Avaris, and introduces the horse-driven chariot (15th and 16th dynasties); the Egyptians still rule on south Egypt, maintaining their capital at Thebes, and Inyotef V founds the 17th dynasty
1532 BC: Ahmose I of Thebes defeats the Hyksos at Avaris and expels them from Egypt
1504 BC: Amenhotep I dies and is succeeded by his brother-in-law Tuthmosis I, who campaigns all the way to Mesopotamia, makes Thebes the most imposing city of the kingdom and erects the Obelisk at the Karnak temple
1458 BC: Tuthmosis III defeats the Mitannis and conquers Syria, the peak of Egyptian power
1300 BC: Egyptians build a canal connecting the Nile and the Red Sea

13 Based on www.scaruffi.com/politics/egyptians.html, Toynbee (1961) and Zhao (2001).

1275 BC: the Egyptian king Rameses II fights against the Hittite king Muwatalli at the city of Kadesh in Syria
926 BC: pharoah Shoshenk invades Palestine
720 BC: the Nubian king Piankh/Piye of Kush (Sudan) conquers the various kingdoms of Egypt and founds the Nubian dynasty
671 BC: the Assyrians defeat Tajarqa and capture the Egyptian capital of Memphis
605 BC: Nebuchadnezzar II leads the Babylonians to conquer Carchemish and defeat the Egyptian army
525 BC: Cambyses of Persia conquers Egypt at the battle of Pelusium
404 BC: Amyrtaios of Sais expels the Persians (28th, 29th and 30th dynasties)
343 BC: the Persians conquer Egypt again (31st dynasty)
332 BC: Alexander the Great conquers Egypt
331 BC: Alexander founds Alexandria in Egypt
196 BC: the Rosetta Stone is carved in both Greek and Egyptian
51 BC: Cleopatra VII Ptolemy becomes queen of Egypt (last of the Greek monarchs)
30 BC: Cleopatra commits suicide and Egypt becomes a province of the Roman empire
395: Egypt is assigned to the eastern Roman empire (Byzantium)
641: Egypt is conquered by the Arabs and forced to convert to Islam

2.4.4 The Indus Valley[14]

2500 BC: farmers with advanced techniques move from far west into the Indus Valley
2000 BC: the Kurgan culture spreads to Eastern Europe and northern Iran
1700 BC: Indo-Iranians migrate eastward to settle in Iran
1600 BC: Indo-Aryans invade India from the northwest and expel the Dravidians
900 BC: Indo-Aryans invade the Ganges valley
521 BC: the Persian empire expands beyond the Indus River (Punjab and Sind)
327 BC: Alexander invades the Indus valley
304 BC: the Magadha king buys the Indus valley for 500 elephants from Seleucus
259 BC: the Mauryan king Ashoka converts to Buddhism and sends out Buddhist missionaries to nearby states
251 BC: Buddhism is introduced to Ceylon (Sri Lanka)
250 BC: Bactria (Afghanistan) declares its independence from the Seleucids
50 AD: Thomas, an apostle of Jesus, visits India
127: Kanishka enlarges his kingdom from Bactria into Uzbekistan, Kashmir and Punjab and promotes Buddhism
233: Ardashir I Sassanid conquers the Kushan empire
510: the Huns led by Mihiragula conquer Punjab, Gujarat and Malwa from the Gupta
528: the Gupta empire collapses under continuous barbaric invasions

[14] Based on www.scaruffi.com/politics/indians.html, Toynbee (1961) and Zhao (2001).

629: the Chinese monk Xuanzang travels to India; Tibet expands to Nepal under Songtsen Gampo
630: Songzen Gampo introduces Buddhism to Bhutan
711: the Arabs conquer Sindh and Multan (Pakistan)
998: Mahmud of Ghazni conquers Punjab
1192: Turkic-speaking chieftains from Afghanistan led by Muhammad of Ghor defeat Prithvi Raj and establish a Muslim sultanate at Delhi
1266: Baban seizes power of the Delhi sultanate and welcomes Islamic refugees fleeing the Mongol hordes the Delhi sultanate
1304: Mongols under Ali Beg invade India but are repelled by the Delhi sultanate
1321: Jordanus, a Dominican monk, is the first Christian missionary in India
1325: Muhammad ibn Tughluq becomes sultan of Delhi
1328: the Mongols invade India but are repelled by the Delhi sultanate
1498: the Portuguese explorer Vasco da Gama reaches India
1509: Portugal conquers Diu and Goa in India; the Vijayanagar kingdom reaches its zenith under Krishna Raja
1526: Babur captures Delhi from Ibrahim, the sultan of Delhi, and founds the Mogul empire in India
1534: Portugal acquires Bombay
1555: the Mogul king Humayun re-conquers India
1600: The British East India Company is established.
1639: Britain acquires Madras from the raja of Chandragiri
1665: Britain acquires Bombay from Portugal
1672: France settles Pondicherry
1686: Mogul emperor Aurangzeb conquers Bijapur, ending the Adil Shahi dynasty
1688: the Moguls complete the conquest of India
1690: Britain acquires Calcutta
1738: Persian general Nader Shah invades India and captures Delhi
1751: Britain becomes the leading colonial power in India
1757: the East India company defeats France and gains access to Bengal
1764: Britain expands to Bengal and Bihar
1776: the Marathas conquer Mysore
1794: the Marathas conquer Delhi

2.5 Summary

'Culture change' is defined as 'the conceptual formulation that refers to the many ways in which societies change their patterns of culture' (Vogt 1972, p. 554). The records of prehistory and history reveal that the patterns of culture of every human society have changed constantly. The rate and type of the cultural change may be slow and gradual, as it was during the Paleolithic, or fast and drastic, as it has been in contemporary societies. Generally, the factors influencing cultural development are diversified—both internally and externally. Internal factors, such as geographical location, natural environment, socioeconomic conditions and technological inventions, may lead to changes in people's lifestyle. External factors, such as immigration, foreign trade and the conquest by another culture, may also bring about culture change. The roles of the internal and external factors in culture change may be different, depending on different space and time conditions.

In this chapter, we have briefly reviewed the evolutions of the world's major civilizations. Our analysis mainly focuses on how these civilizations were interacted with each other. We have also presented details about their dynamic relations with the rest of the world. A host of factors, including, *inter alia*, immigration, increased diplomatic and cultural contacts, the diffusion of science and technology, the mass media and international travel and trade, are dramatically transforming contemporary international political and economic relations. As a result the interactions between different cultures are becoming more and more important in our changing world.

Since the end of the Cold War, the study of intercultural relations has become a popular topic in the field of global politics and economics. But support has been found for views emphasizing both intercultural conflict and cooperation. With all the positive ways of gaining from intercultural cooperation, it seems logical to inquire why economic cooperation has failed. Regions are a basis for cooperation among states only to the extent that geography coincides with culture. Divorced from culture, propinquity does not yield commonality and may foster just the reverse. The overall effectiveness of multicultural organizations generally varies inversely with the cultural diversity among their members. As a result single cultural organizations are more stable and successful than multicultural organizations. This is true for both political and economic organizations.

Box 2.1 Why prairie and steppe nomads became different

The North American Prairie nomads and the Eurasian Steppe nomads are thought to have been blood relatives. At least 12,000 years ago, The Prairie nomads crossed the Bering land bridge and settled at the North America. The end of the nomadic era came around the same time for both groups when Europeans and Euro-Americans invaded their territories and brought with them the five-fold threat of disease, firearms, immigration, agriculture and formidable administration.

The Eurasian Steppe nomads bordered the Near Eastern, Mesopotamian, Indus and Chinese civilizations, which produced inventions such as the wheel and the smelting furnace. As a result the Steppe nomads enjoyed the benefits of those inventions, and had early access to the horse as a beast of burden and a means of transportation. The Prairie nomads lived far from the advanced civilizations of Mesoamerica and received little influence from them. Prairie nomads had only the dog and there is no evidence of the wheel on the ancient Plains. Steppe nomads therefore traveled greater distances with heavier loads than Prairie nomads.

Although the human population in both regions was relatively small and thinly dispersed, which was limited by the availability of food and water, especially during the frequent periods of drought, the Steppe nomads were much stronger than the Prairie nomads. About 190,000 individuals populated the Plains. On the Steppes, the average population was probably ten times larger, and the nomadic tribes sometimes came together to form major empires.

Source Based on CMCC (2006)

References

Barro RJ, Sala-i-Martin X (1995) Economic growth. McGraw-Hill, New York

Bauman Z (1999) Culture as praxis. Sage Publications, London and New York

Braudel F (1981) The structure of everyday life, civilization and capitalism 15-18th Century, vol. 1. Harper and Row, New York

Brezis E, Krugman P, Tsiddon D (1993) Leapfrogging in international competition: a theory of cycles in national technological leadership. Am Econ Rev 83(3):1211–1219

CMCC (2006) Masters of the plains: Ancient nomads of Russia and Canada (Prairie vs. Steppe Nomads: Similar, or different?), Canadian Museum of civilization Cooperation. Available. www.civilization.ca/cmc/maitres/masters04e.html. Accessed 10 Oct 2007

Coppa A, Bondioli L, Cucina A, Frayer DW, Jarrige C (2006) Early neolithic tradition of dentistry: flint tips were surprisingly effective for drilling tooth enamel in a prehistoric population. Nature 440:755. doi:10.1038/440755a

Dai Y, Gong S (ed) (2000) A history of China (zhongguo tongshi), a four-volume edition. Haiyan Press (in Chinese), Zhengzhou

Frankel JA, Stein E, Wei S-J (1997) Trading blocs and the Americas: the natural, the Unnatural, and the super-natural. J Dev Econ 47(1):61–95

Guo R (2009) Intercultural economic analysis—theory and method. Springer, New York

Huntington SP (1993) The clash of civilizations? Foreign Aff 71(Summer):2–32

International Monetary Fund (1997) World Economic Outlook, May. Washington DC: the IMF

Jovanovic B, Nyakro Y (1994) The Bayesian foundations of learning by doing. Unpublished paper, New York University, New York

Kanamori T, Motohashi K (2007) Information technology and economic growth: comparison between Japan and Korea. RIETI discussion paper series 07-E-009. Research Institute of Economy, Trade and Industry (RIETI), Tokyo

Kolars JF, Mitchell W (1991) The Euphrates River and the Southeast Anatolia development project. Carbondale and Edwardsville, Illinois, Southern Illinois University Press

Landes D (1966) Technological change and development in Western Europe. In: Habakkuk H, Posten M (eds) The Cambridge economic history of Europe, vol. 6. Cambridge University Press, Cambridge, pp 1750–1914

Levine DN (1972) Cultural integration. In Sillis DL (ed) International Encyclopedia of the social sciences, vol. 3. The Macmillan Company & The Free Press, New York pp 372–80

Maddison A (2001) The world economy: a millennial perspective. OECD Development Center, Paris

Sapir E (1949) Selected writings in language, culture, and personality. In: Mandelbaum DG (ed). University of California Press, Berkeley

Toynbee A (1961) A study of history. Oxford University Press, London
Vogt EE (1972) Culture change. In: Sillis DL (ed) International Encyclopedia of the social sciences, vol. 3. The Macmillan Company & The Free Press, New York, pp 554–8
Weber M (1904, 1930) The protestant ethic and the spirit of capitalism. Allen & Unwin, London
Zhao F (ed) (2001) A history of the world (a ten-volume edition). Beifang Funvertong Press (in Chinese), Changchun

Chapter 3
Intercultural Economic Influences

Abstract Given the markedly differing attitudes as well as cultural values between different cultural groups of people, the adoption of a common standard is unlikely to prove effective. However 'cultural dissimilarity' may also generate 'economic complementarities' that will in turn exert positive influences on foreign trade. As a result the final output of the cultural influences should be nonlinear, subjecting to various conditions concerned. In this chapter, cultural influences on international trade are found to be more significant for the post-Cold War era than in the Cold War era. Our empirical results also provide evidence supporting the presumption that high-income trade partners will be less sensitive to the measures of cultural dissimilarity than low-income trade partners between which cultural dissimilarity leads to barriers to international trade. The treatment of linguistic and religious factors as continuous variables in this chapter has improved past studies in which 'language' was treated as one or more dummy variables and 'religion' was ignored.

Keywords Spatial adjacency · Cultural similarity · Intercultural trade · Intercultural influence · Gravity model

3.1 Literature Review

It has been broadly assumed that a country's foreign economic dependence on the outside world is negatively related to its land area. For example, in an estimation of international trade, Frankel and Romer (1996, Table 1) find that, for every 1% increase in land area, trade falls by about 0.2% accordingly. This may be illustrated unambiguously by the relationship between the supply and demand of some basic resources for countries differing in size (land area). Generally speaking, in comparison to large economies, small economies have a relatively limited variety of natural resources. Therefore, they have to import resources that they lack and that

R. Guo, *Introduction to Intercultural Economics*, SpringerBriefs in Economics,
DOI: 10.1007/978-3-642-29276-7_3, © The Author(s) 2012

are essential to meeting diversified production and consumption needs. Eventually, the increased imports will stimulate exports in order to attain a balance.

Besides geographical space, a country's economic size (output) and population also influence its foreign trade. Generally, the larger the GDPs (or GNPs)[1] of trading partners, *ceteris paribus*, the larger the volume of trade between them; by contrast, population is a negative factor in the determination of international trade. This captures the well-known phenomenon that larger countries tend to be relatively less open to trade as a percentage of GDP (or GNP). Therefore, it is easy to understand that Hong Kong, Singapore and Luxembourg are more highly dependent on international trade than the United States, China or India. The former economies lack not only natural endowments but also room to exploit economies of scale in the domestic market, while the latter, engaging in far more trade in absolute terms (*versus* less trade as a percentage of GDP or GNP), can find more business opportunities inside their own territories.

Past studies on the geographical influence on trade have raised more questions than they answered. For example, among the existing estimated results on the determinants of international trade (in logarithmic form), the statistically significant coefficients on the log of distance have ranged between –0.51 and –1.50, which demonstrates the respective decreases (in percentage) in international trade as a result of a 1% increase in distance.[2] No observable tendency, however, has been found for the effect of geographical proximity to fall over time. Rather, the trend seems to be upward during the courses of, among others, 1950–1988 in Boisso and Ferrantino (1997) and 1965–1992 in Frankel et al. (1997b). In their analyses on the negative correlation between distance and the interdependence for sovereign countries, Frankel et al. (1997a) use the data from the 1980s and obtain slightly larger coefficients (around 0.5–0.6) on distance compared with Eichengreen and Irwin's (1995) interwar estimates (around 0.3–0.6) based on the data of the 1930s. Similarly, based on the panel data from 1970, 1980 and 1990, Rauch's (1999) results show little evidence to support the decreasing tendency for trade with respect to distance from 1970 to 1990. Clearly this does not provide evidence that, as a result of declining transportation cost, there should have a decreasingly negative relation between trade and distance. Intuitively, we suspect that some powerful explanatory variables that may either resist or aid international trade must have been missing or simplified, which could in turn reduce to a greater or lesser extent the reliability of the estimated results.

Past theories on the determinants of international trade seem controversial, or at least incomplete. The Heckscher–Ohlin (H–O), or factor-endowment, theory can be expressed in terms of two theorems. According to the H–O theorem, a nation will export the commodity produced by relatively abundant and cheap factor and

---

[1] Linnemann (1966) and Frankel et al. (1997a) have estimated the effects of both GDP and GNP on trade, but no significant difference is found.

[2] For example, Linnemann (1966) puts the estimated coefficient as –0.77, Brada and Mendez (1983) and Oguledo and MacPhee (1994) as 0.76, Bikker (1987) as –0.90 to –1.1, Mansfield and Bronson (1997) as –0.51 to –0.69 (for 1950–90), and Rauch (1999) as –0.62 to –0.70 (1970–90).

import the commodity produced by relatively scarce and expensive factor (see Heckscher 1919; Ohlin 1933). The factor-price equalization theorem was rigorously proved by P.A. Samuelson and therefore is also called Heckscher–Ohlin–Samuelson (H–O–S) theorem (Samuelson 1948, 1949). According to the H–O–S theorem, international trade will bring about equalization in the relative and absolute returns to homogeneous factors across nations. The first empirical test of the H–O model was conducted by Leontief (1954) using 1947 US data, which demonstrates that US import substitutes were about 30% more capital-intensive than US exports. Since the United States is the most capital-intensive nation, this result was the opposite of what the H–O model predicted and became known as Leontief paradox. This paradox could be explained by (1) 1947 being a nonrepresentative year, (2) the use of a two-factor (labor and capital) model, (3) the fact that US tariffs gave more protection to labor-intensive industries, and (4) the exclusion of human capital from the calculations. Some empirical studies, however, give conflicting results.[3]

A more uniform size distribution among economies is one explanation for the increase in global trade. Moreover, Helpman (1987) and Krugman (1995) predict that if the distribution of national incomes across countries becomes more equal over time, the volume of trade should increase. According to the Krugman–Helpman theory, the sum of the logs of per capita GNPs of two countries will have a positive effect on the log form of trade between the two countries. One possible explanation for the independent effect of income per capita is that exotic foreign varieties are superior goods in consumption. Low-income countries are dominated by subsistence farming. Other possibilities come out of the literature relating to endogenous theory on economic growth.[4] Even though more developed countries have more advanced transportation infrastructures, including seaports and airports, which facilitate trade, Frankel et al. (1997b) argue that perhaps the most important reason why industrialized countries trade more than the less developed countries is that countries tend to liberate as they develop. One reason for this pattern is that governments of poor countries depend on tariff revenue for a large portionof their budget, while more advanced countries can apply other forms of direct and indirect taxes to the domestic economy.

Till now, it seems that there should have been different hypotheses on the correlation between income level and volume of trade. Markusen (1986) and Deardorff (1998, p. 15), for example, show that if high-income consumers tend to consume larger budget shares of capital-intensive goods, which, according to the H–O theory, are produced by capital-rich countries, then it follows that (1) capital-rich countries will trade more with other capital-rich countries than with

---

[3] See, for example, Leontief (1956), Kravis (1956a, b), Keesing (1966), Kenen (1965), Baldwin (1971), Branson and Monoyios (1977), Leamer (1980, 1984, 1993), Stern and Maskus (1981), Bowen et al. (1987), and Salvatore and Barazesh (1990).

[4] Frankel et al. (1997a, p. 58). Of the many relevant works, some of the more important are Grossman and Helpman (1989, 1991), Rivera-Batiz and Romer (1991) and, for further references on the connections between trade and growth, Frankel et al. (1995).

capital-poor countries, and (2) capital-poor countries will trade more with other capital-poor countries than with capital-rich countries. Obviously, these arguments support the results of Linder (1961), Helpman (1987) and, more recently, Krugman (1995) but not that of the H–O theory.

The classical theory does not offer a satisfactory explanation of why production conditions differ between countries. This is perhaps not surprising, given the nature of production at that time. Resource and cost differences were taken as given and as part of the environment in which the economic system functioned. The underlying cost differences were viewed as being determined outside the economic system for the most part, governed by the natural endowment of a country's resources. The theory does, however, make it clear that even if a country is absolutely more or less efficient in the production of all commodities, a basis for trade still exists if there is a difference in the degree of relative efficiency across commodities. Thus, there is a basis for trade between a developing country and an industrialized country that is more efficient in the production of all commodities. Both can benefit from specialization in production and trade of those commodities in which each has a comparative advantage.

The H–O theory has left a great deal of today's international trade unexplained. To fill up this gap, economists have put forward new theories that base international trade on economies of scale, imperfection, and cross-national differences in technological changes, among others. Even though two nations are identical in every respect, there is still a basis for mutually beneficial trade based on economies of scale. When each nation specializes in the production of one commodity, the combined total world output of both commodities will be greater than without specialization when economies of scale are present. A large portion of international trade today involves the exchange of differentiated products. Such intra-industry trade arises in order to take advantage of important economies of scale in production. Studies show that the more similar nations are in factor endowments, the greater is the importance of intra-industry relative to inter-industry trade.[5] According to the technological gap model, a firm exports a new product until imitators in other countries take its market away. In the meantime, the imitation lag allows delays in the diffusion of technology across national borders. The product cycle theory that relaxes several assumptions in the traditional trade theories defines that a product goes through five stages, including the introduction of the product, expansion of production for export, standardization and beginning of production abroad through imitation, foreign imitators underselling the nation in third markets, and foreigners underselling the innovating firms in their home markets as well (Salvatore 1995, p. 176).

To sum up, current trade theories seem incomplete and, sometimes, controversial, especially when trade partners with different cultural characteristics are taken into account. They cannot be used to explain satisfactorily why world

[5] Selected literature on the intra-industry trade can be found in Grubel and Lloyd (1975), Krugman (1980), Lancaster (1980), Greenaway and Milner (1986), Vona (1990), and Leamer (1993).

economic activities in the same or similar cultural environments have become increasingly more important, while the opposite is true of partners in cross-cultural environment; neither can they provide a clear and concrete methodology to explain the extraordinary trade performances within the Chinese cultural circle (Taiwan, Hong Kong, Macau, mainland China and other Chinese areas) during the post-Cold War period. Furthermore, the following are still more puzzling the international economic theorists and practitioners: Why has Germany attracted much less foreign direct investment (FDI) than the UK? Why has France achieved a better foreign trade performance than Italy?

3.2 Doing Business Across Cultures

The emphasis on the role of cultural linkage in foreign trade can be traced back to biological analyses showing that cooperation among animals is influenced by genetic similarity (Wilson 1980). Although it is not the only tool with which to build trusting relationships, businessmen usually make deals with whom they can understand. By contrast, minority faces disadvantages in conducting intercultural economic activities.[6] Trade and economic cooperation are based on cultural commonality, as it is easier and more efficient for people with the same cultural identity (language, religion, or any other cultural element) to trust and communicate with each other than for those with different cultural identities.

Since the adoption of a common standard between different cultural groups of people is not likely, given that they have markedly differing attitudes as well as different cultural values, the greater the cultural difference involved in a multi-cultural society, the higher the managerial risks and costs resulting from it. The problems inherent in intracultural and intercultural behaviors can be summarized as follows (Huntington 1996, p. 129):

- feelings of superiority (and occasionally inferiority) toward people who are perceived as being very different;
- fear of and lack of trust in such people;
- communication difficulties resulting from differences in language and accepted civil behavior;
- lack of familiarity with the assumptions, motivations, relationships and social practices of other people.

For a long time since the World War II, the influences of various cultural factors on economic activities had been ignored by the mainstream development thinkers and practitioners. It seems probably that these conclusions could be correct under certain circumstances. During the Cold War, ideological preferences

[6] We define 'intercultural trade' as 'trade between countries or regions differing in one or more cultural elements'. However, since no countries have exactly same cultural elements, 'intercultural trade' and 'international trade' are not different from each other.

might have been of greatest significance in decision-making (Huntington 1996, p. 125). Consequently, the cultural determinants of the international trade of the Cold War might be different from that of the post-Cold War period.

Since the end of the Cold War, there has been a growing concern that cultural links exhibit a trend towards increasing trade between countries that are similar to each other culturally (see Rauch and Trindade 2002, among others). Trade within the European Community constituted less than 50% of the community's total trade before the 1980s; by the 1990s this has grown to more than 60%. Trade among the ASEAN, Taiwan, Hong Kong, South Korea and the mainland of China—most of which either fall within or are closely related to the Chinese cultural circle—increased from less than 10% to over 30% of total trade from the 1950s to the 1990s. Similar shifts toward intraregional trade also occurred in Latin America in the 1990s, with trade between Brazil and Argentina tripling and Colombia-Venezuela trade quadrupling between 1990 and 1993. In 1994 Brazil replaced the United States as Argentina's principal trading partner.[7]

By way of contrast, there is a quite different viewpoint, showing that the direction of the correlation between cultural dissimilarity and international trade may change under different conditions. In order to quantitatively investigate the nonlinear effects of culture on international trade, one may build empirical models in which cultural linkage is designed not only as an individual explanatory variable but also as a product with income level. If these explanatory variables are statistically significantly when estimated simultaneously, one can further divide the full samples into two groups (that is, one with low income level trade partners, and one with high income level trade partners) under which cultural influences on international trade can be estimated, respectively. On this basis and using panel data from the USA and China, cultural influences on foreign trade are found to have two different directions during the 1990s: cultural dissimilarity tends to retard trade with poor countries and regions and to encourage trade with richer economies (Guo 2004).

In the analysis of bilateral trade and economic cooperation, economists have taken account of resource endowment including quantity of arable land, quality of the soil, presence of natural resources and climate, as well as labor and managerial skills and organizational capacity. But little attention has been paid to cultural differences that would not only decide the characteristics of social resources but also influence trade patterns, either directly or indirectly. As a matter of fact, in addition to the fact that intercultural differences generate some managing risks and extra costs for bilateral trade, intercultural trade is important not only for the realization of economies of scale but also for the utilization of the culturally based complementary conditions (see Box 3.1). Although every cultural group runs the risk of being stereotyped because of shared commonalities, no group, culture, or person remains static or lives in isolation. Instead, all societies have interacted. History reveals similarities in societal structures, and differences in behavior and

[7] *Data source*: IMF (various issues).

stages of development. The diversity and plurality of cultures can and do benefit from each other, as cultures discover their own peculiarities and idiosyncrasies.

Box 3.1 Comparative Cultural Advantages

Culture plays differing roles in the formation of intercultural relations. On the one hand, cultural dissimilarity brings about extra costs and risks in cross-cultural communication. On the other hand, it generates 'differentiation of production' or economic complementarity, which in turn induces cooperation among distinctive groups of people. From the perspective of comparative economics, 'differentiation of production' implies 'comparative advantages', while the latter influences to some extent the potential benefit of trade and cooperation between different cultures.

The term 'cultural monopolization of trade' denotes that, since there are usually some culturally unique–both traditional and modern–commodities in each culture, intercultural exporters of these products can realize a monopolized profit for each of their own. As a result, one culture's gross benefit of exporting its products to the other culture grows with greater degree of intercultural dissimilarity. As a result cultural dissimilarity is a determining source not only for intercultural conflicts but also for intercultural dependence and cooperation.

Keeping in mind that there are different viewpoints on cultural influences on trade, it is therefore worth to note that the changing roles that culture plays in trade are very sensitive to various conditions. In order to make the analysis clearer and more concrete, some assumptions are necessary. The market structure is one of imperfect competition, with oligopolistic firms producing goods that are perfect substitutes for each other. It is assumed that the markets are segmented in different areas. In addition, we further assume that:

1. There are two factors affecting trade, that is, benefit of economic complementarity and cost of inter-political and intercultural barriers.
2. Technology is identical in all culture areas, that is, trade functions are the same in all culture areas.
3. All commodities are produced under constant returns to scale in all culture areas.
4. There is no intercultural factor mobility.
5. There are no transportation costs, tariffs, or other obstructions to the free flow of trade.
6. Trade between the culture areas concerned is balanced.

The meaning of assumption 1 is clear, and it is made to simplify the illustration. Assumption 2 means that all culture areas have access to and use the same general production techniques. Since factor prices usually differ, each culture area will use more of the relatively cheaper factor in the culture area so as to minimize its costs of production and intercultural trade. Assumption 3 means that increasing the amount of labor and capital used in the production of any commodity will increase output of that commodity in the same production. Assumption 4 means that intercultural differences in factor earnings would persist indefinitely in the absence of intercultural trade. Assumption 5 means that specialization in production proceeds until commodity prices are the same in both culture areas with trade. If we allowed for transportation costs and tariffs, specialization would proceed only until commodity prices differed by no more than the costs of transportation and the tariff on each unit of the interculturally traded commodity. Lastly, assumption 6 means that the total value of each culture area's exports equals the total value of the area's imports.

The analytical framework can be further simplified. Assume that in a pair of economically complementary nations, the size of their bilateral trade is jointly determined by only two factors: (1) the cost of intercultural transaction (c) and (2) the benefit of comparative advantage (b). Specifically, trade is supposed throughout this research to be encouraged for $b > c$ and to be retarded for other circumstances. On this basis, there is always a negative relation between the cost of intercultural transaction and cultural similarity. To enable the analytical framework concrete, we suppose that the function c is monotonously related to cultural similarity (x), that is,

$$c = c(x), \text{ with } c'(x) < 0 \text{ and } c''(x) = 0.$$

In all circumstances, $b(x)$ is positive for economically complementary nations, that is,

$$b(x) > 0 \quad \text{for all x.}$$

However, the marginal benefit of comparative advantage with respect to cultural similarity, denoted by db/dx, may be positive, negative or zero. Finally, we have Hypothesis 1 for the cultural conditions under which trade is encouraged or retarded:

(a) When $db/dx > 0$, trade tends to be retarded for values of cultural similarity to be less than x^* and to be encouraged otherwise (see Fig. 3.1a).
(b) When $db/dx \leq 0$, trade tends to be retarded for values of cultural similarity to be less than x_1^* and to be encouraged otherwise if $|db/dx| < |dc/dx|$; it tends to be encouraged for values of cultural similarity to be less than x_2^* and to be retarded otherwise if $|db/dx| > |dc/dx|$ (see Fig. 3.1b).
(c) When $db/dx = dc/dx$, trade tends to be retarded if $b < c$ for all values of cultural similarity and to be encouraged if $b > c$ for all values of cultural similarity (see Fig. 3.1c).

Next, let us add another explanatory variable, income level (y), into the system in which cultural similarity is fixed at a certain level. It is further assumed that,

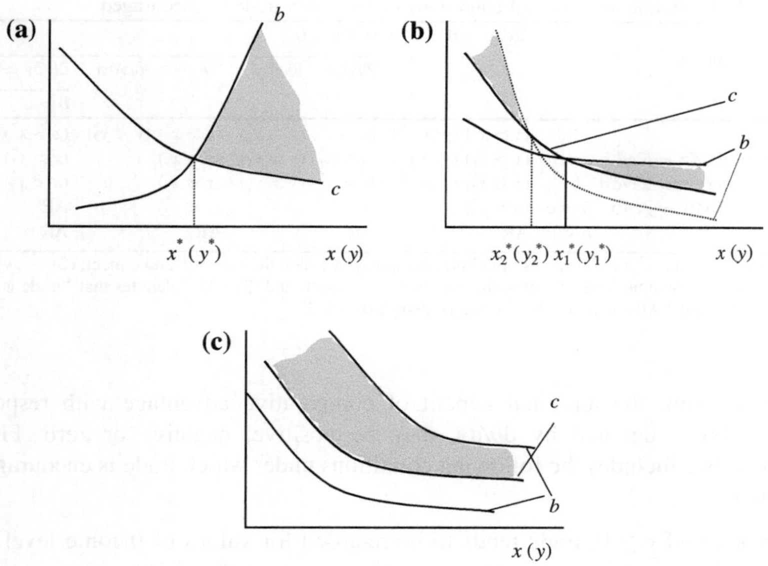

Fig. 3.1 Conditions under which trade is encouraged

ceteris paribus, the cost of intercultural transaction is negatively related to income level. Perhaps the most obvious evidence that supports this view is the decreasing transportation cost as a result of economic development, not to mention that the higher the education attainment (which is positively related to income level), the easier is it for people from different cultural backgrounds to communicate with and understand each other. The functions of the cost of intercultural transaction and the benefit of comparative advantage, now, becomes

$$b = b(x, y); c = c(x, y), \quad \text{with } \partial c/\partial y < 0.$$

In a check on the relation between the benefit of comparative advantage and income level, there may be different scenarios. First of all, there is an indication that the benefit of comparative advantage increases with higher income level. This viewpoint has been confirmed by the empirical analyses of, among others, Helpman (1987) and Krugman (1995), in which the sum of the logs of per capita GNPs of two countries will have a positive effect on the log form of trade between the two countries. Second, there may be a negative relation between the benefit of comparative advantage and income level, as indicated in some empirical results (Rauch 1999).[8]

[8] As a matter of fact, a negative coefficient on per capita GDP sometimes may be found in gravity model on trade for homogeneous products if they are more agricultural and rich countries tend to have managed trade in agricultural products.

Table 3.1 Economic and cultural conditions under which trade is encouraged

Income level / Cultural similarity	$\partial b/\partial y \geq 0$	$\partial b/\partial y < 0$			
		$\lvert\partial b/\partial y\rvert < \lvert\partial c/\partial y\rvert$	$\lvert\partial b/\partial y\rvert > \lvert\partial c/\partial y\rvert$	$\partial b/\partial y = \partial c/\partial y$	
				$b > c$	$b < c$
$\partial b/\partial x \geq 0$	$(x > x^*)\ (y > y^*)$	$(x > x^*)\ (y > y_1^*)$	$(x > x^*)\ (y < y_2^*)$	$(x > x^*)$	AR
$\partial b/\partial x < 0$ $\lvert\partial b/\partial x\rvert < \lvert\partial c/\partial x\rvert$	$(x > x_1^*)\ (y > y^*)$	$(x > x_1^*)\ (y > y_1^*)$	$(x > x_1^*)$	$(x > x_1^*)$	AR
$\lvert\partial b/\partial x\rvert > \lvert\partial c/\partial x\rvert$	$(x < x_2^*)\ (y > y^*)$	$(x < x_2^*)\ (y > y_1^*)$	$(x < x_2^*)$	$(x < x_2^*)$	AR
$\partial b/\partial x = \partial c/\partial x$ $b > c$	$(y > y^*)$	$(y > y_1^*)$	$(y < y_2^*)$	AE	AR
$b < c$	AR	AR	AR	AR	AR

Notes (1) x^*, x_1^* and x_2^* are the values of cultural similarity at which the curves *b* and *c* meet; (2) y^*, y_1^* and y_2^* are the values of income level at which the curves *b* and *c* meet; and (3) "AE" denotes that "trade is always encouraged", and "AR" denotes that "trade is always retarded"

As a result, the marginal benefit of comparative advantage with respect to income level, denoted by d*b*/d*y*, may be positive, negative or zero. Finally, Hypothesis 2 includes the following conditions under which trade is encouraged or retarded:

(a) When $\partial b/\partial y \geq 0$, trade tends to be retarded for values of income level to be less than y^* and to be encouraged otherwise (see Fig. 3.1a).
(b) When $\partial b/\partial y < 0$, trade tends to be retarded for values of income level to be less than y_1^* and to be encouraged otherwise if $\lvert\partial b/\partial y < \lvert\partial c/\partial y\rvert$; it tends to be encouraged for values of income level to be less than y_2^* and to be retarded otherwise if $\lvert\partial b/\partial y > \lvert\partial c/\partial y\rvert$ (see Fig. 3.1b).
(c) When $\partial b/\partial y = \partial c/\partial y$, trade tends to be retarded if $b < c$ for all values of income level and to be encouraged if $b > c$ for all values of income level (see Fig. 3.1c).

After combining Hypotheses 1 and 2 together, we may have the cultural and economic conditions under which trade is encouraged or retarded (see Table 3.1).

3.3 A Gravity Model of Trade

Among the quantitative studies of international trade and economic cooperation, gravity model is the tool most commonly used by economists.[9] The most classic and extensive early application of the model was by Linnemann (1966), who continued work first reported in Tinbergen (1962) and then in Pöyhönen (1963). The most recent work on the application of the gravity model was Frankel et al. (1997b), Deardorff (1998), Rauch (1999), Rose (2004), among others. Generally, a gravity model assumes that the size of bilateral economic activities between any

[9] The application of the gravity model in regional science and economic geography can be traced back to as far as the 1940s (see, for example, Zipf 1946; Stewart 1948; and Isard 1949).

two countries depends on both the product of the economic sizes of the countries and the distance between them. In addition, income level as well as whether or not a country-pair shares a common land border have also considered as standard covariates in the gravity model of international economic trade.

In order to test the effects of the various cultural variables on international trade, we control other political and social variables. Instead, we introduce a set of cultural similarity variables—represented by SIMILARITY. Although the components of culture have been variously defined, we have focused on only two elements—language and religion. Of course, our discussion of these cultural elements is not definitive and perhaps would not satisfy anthropologists. Nevertheless, our consideration is due to the concerns that 'language' is an effective tool of communication and that 'religion' can provide the insights into the characteristics of culture. To control for the countries' propensity to foreign economic activities, we use some dummies for the selected countries. Let us first consider a basic form of gravity model:

$$\begin{aligned}\ln(\text{TRADE}_{ij}+1) = \alpha_0 + \alpha_1 \ln(\text{GNP}_i\text{GNP}_j) + \alpha_2 \ln\text{DISTANCE}_{ij} \\ + \alpha_3\text{ADJACENT}_{ij} + \alpha_4\text{SIMILARITY}_{ij} \\ + \Sigma\alpha_{5+k}\text{COUNTRY}_k \end{aligned} \tag{3.1}$$

In Eq. (3.1), 'ln' represents natural logarithm; TRADE_{ij} denotes nominal bilateral trade between countries (regions) i and j (in thousand US dollars). In order to make the natural logarithm of TRADE become mathematically meaningful when TRADE = 0,[10] we use ln(TRADE + 1) to approximately denote ln(TRADE). This seems to be reasonable since the size of TRADE (measured in thousand US dollars is) is, if not zero, always far larger than 1).[11] GNP_iGNP_j is the product of nominal GNPs of the ith and jth countries (regions) (all in thousand US dollars). DISTANCE_{ij} represents the distance between the geographical centers of the ith and jth countries (regions) (in kilometers); and ADJACENT_{ij} is a dummy variable, which takes the value of '1' for countries (regions) i and j to have a common border and '0' otherwise. According to the past studies, we expect the estimated coefficients on the above variables to follow: $\alpha_1 > 0$, $\alpha_2 < 0$, and $\alpha_3 > 0$. COUNTRY_k denotes the dummy of the kth country.

Calculation of the distance between trade partners must require some elaboration here. Most existing studies like using the distance between two major cities to denote the proximity between the two trade partners. The cities are either the capitals or economic centers.[12] Another method is to use the geographical centers

---

[10] Note that if there are a significant number of zero values in the pair-wise trade, then Tobit regressions techniques should be used. However, in this research, the number of country-pairs identified by 'TRADE = 0' (that is, there is no trade for a country pair) is quite small.

[11] In fact, there still exist some amount of 'illegal' (or unofficial) trade for those economies that are officially reporting no bilateral trade flows.

[12] For example, Frankel et al. (1997a, p. 56) use Chicago for the major city of the United States rather than Washington, DC, and Shanghai for the major city of China rather than Beijing.

to measure the distance between the trade partners. According to Boisso and Ferrantino (1997), there is little difference in whether distance is measured between the most populous cities or the geographical centers. The last method, which has been applied by Linnemann (1966), Eichengreen and Irwin (1995), and others, use distance measured 'as the crow files'—what is technically called the great-circle distance between the two latitude-longitude combinations.

Previous studies, such as Frankel et al. (1995 and 1997b), also use dummies for 'membership' in the geographical areas of East Asia, Western Hemisphere, and so on. Including these dummy variables could, as stated by Rauch (1999, fn. 6), shrink the estimated coefficients on 'distance'. The reason why the dummies for membership in the geographical areas are excluded from Eq. (3.1) is additionally due to the fact that they could compound the problem of interpretation that will be presented by the cultural variables employed.

We are now most interested in the cultural factors that may resist or aid international trade. To go further, we use SIMILARITY_{ij} to express the extent to which the ith and jth trade partners are culturally linked each other (details about the measurement will be discussed later). Technically, if the cultural variable is statistically insignificant in Eq. (3.1), there might exist some possibility for the existence of other form(s) of relationship between international trade and cultural similarity. To investigate the nonlinear relationship, we add a new variable: $\ln(\text{GNPPC}_i\text{GNPPC}_j)$, where $\ln(\text{GNPPC}_i\text{GNPPC}_j)$ is the natural log of the per capita GNP (in nominal US dollars) of the ith and jth trade partners. The effect of the SIMILARITY index on international trade is now allowed to depend on the level of economic development, measured by per capita GNP. The SIMILARITY variable is now entered into the gravity model of trade linearly and also as a product with the natural log of per capita GNP. Consequently, we have a modified form of gravity model:

$$\begin{aligned}\ln\left(\text{TRADE}_{ij}+1\right) = \beta_0 &+ \beta_1\ln\left(\text{GNP}_i\text{GNP}_j\right) + \beta_2\ln\text{DISTANCE}_{ij}\\ &+ \beta_3\text{ADJACENT}_{ij} + \beta_4\text{SIMILARITY}_{ij}\\ &+ \beta_5\text{SIMILARITY}_{ij}\ln\left(\text{GNPPC}_i\text{GNPPC}_j\right)\\ &+ \Sigma\beta_{6+k}\text{COUNTRY}_k\end{aligned} \tag{3.2}$$

In Eq. (3.2), if the estimated coefficients on SIMILARITY_{ij} (that is, β_4) and on $\text{SIMILARITY}_{ij}\ln(\text{GNPPC}_i\text{GNPPC}_j)$ (that is, β_5) have different signs (such as $\beta_4 > 0$ and $\beta_5 < 0$; or $\beta_4 < 0$ and $\beta_5 > 0$) and are statistically significant, we obtain a breakpoint value ($\text{GNPPC}_i\text{GNPPC}_j^*$) by letting the first-order differentials of the dependent variable ($\ln(\text{TRADE}_{ij} + 1)$ with respect to SIMILARITY be zero, that is, $\text{GNPPC}_i\text{GNPPC}_j^* = \exp(-\beta_{4/}\beta_5)$. Specifically, as for the case $\beta_4 > 0$ and $\beta_5 < 0$, we have

(i) The effect of cultural similarity on international trade is positive if the income level of the ith and jth trade partners ($\text{GNPPC}_i\text{GNPPC}_j$) is less than $\text{GNPPC}_i\text{GNPPC}_j{}^*$;

(ii) The effect of cultural similarity on international trade is negative if the income level of the *i*th and *j*th trade partners ($GNPPC_iGNPPC_j$) is more than $GNPPC_iGNPPC_j{}^*$.

Our particular concern is that since the 1990s, the old environment of the Cold War era has been replaced by the emergence of a new economic regionalism. As a result nations have been reshuffling their relations with the rest of the world. They have been during the post-Cold War era groping for groupings, and they are finding those groupings with countries of similar economic and cultural interests, while abandoning or peeling off those groupings with countries of different economic and cultural interests (Huntington 1996, p. 125). In order to quantitatively investigate the effects of cultural influences on international trade, we use the recent data of a panel of nations. Since international trade performance might differ between the Cold War and the post-Cold War periods, we select two years—1990 (representing the Cold War period) and 2000 (representing the post-Cold War period).[13]

Linguistic and religious similarity indexes can be constructed in different ways. The simplest method is to use a dummy index; i.e., using '1' for economies to be linguistically and religiously linked with each other, and using '0' otherwise. Although it has been applied in a number of studies (see, for example, Havrylyshyn and Pritchett 1991; Foroutan and Pritchett 1993; Frankel and Wei 1995; Frankel et al. 1997b), this method cannot precisely measure the extent to which economies are linguistically and religiously linked each other, particularly when the economies are linguistically and religiously diversified. In this research, a comprehensive method is used to construct linguistic and religious similarity indexes. Suppose that the population shares of N cultural (linguistic, religious) groups are expressed by $(x_1, x_2,\ldots, x_N)$ and $(y_1, y_2,\ldots, y_N)$ for economies X and Y, respectively. x_i and y_i (where, $x_i \geq 0$ and $y_i \geq 0$) belong to the same linguistic (religious) group. Mathematically, the linguistic and religious similarity indexes (denoted by LANGUAGE and RELIGION, respectively) between the economies X and Y can be measured according to the following formula:

$$\sum\nolimits_{i=1}^{N} \min(x_i, y_i) \tag{3.3}$$

In Eq. (3.3), min (•) denotes the minimization of the variables within parentheses. The values of LANGUAGE and RELIGION range between 0 and 1. In the extreme cases, when LANGUAGE (RELIGION) = 1, the two economies have a common linguistic (religious) structure (i.e., for all i, $x_i = y_i$); when LANGUAGE (RELIGION) = 0, the two economies do not have any linguistic (religious) links with each other (i.e., for all i, x_i (or y_i) = 0 and $x_i \neq y_i$). In the other words, greater values of LANGUAGE or RELIGION indicate greater linguistic or religious similarity between two economies. This formula has been used in Guo

[13] Technically, the data of more years should be considered to represent each period. But this would increase the difficulties in the collection and calculation of cultural data.

(2004, 2006) and Noland (2005). Several other methods can also be used to comprehensively measure linguistic and religious similarity indexes. Boisso and Ferrantino (1997), for example, use $\sum x_i y_i$ as the construct of similarity index. However, using Eq. (3.3) can prevent the index from further reduction when the values of x_i and y_i are small.

To quantitatively investigate and compare the cultural influences on international trade during the Cold War and the post-Cold War periods, we will use the panel data for two years (1990 and 2000). In each year Brazil, China, Dem. Rep. of Congo (or Zaire for 1990), France, Germany (or West Germany for 1990), India, Japan, Russia (or USSR for 1990), Saudi Arabia, and the United States are chosen. The reason why we choose the ten countries is due to the concern that not only they have encompassed most of the world economy and population, but also each of them represents a major language and/or religion of the world.[14] In sum, the languages to be considered are Amharic, Arabic, Armenian, Bengali, Chinese, Czech, Danish, Dutch, English, Finnish, French, German, Greek, Hebrew, Hindi, Hungarian, Italian, Japanese, Kazak, Korean, Kyrgyz, Miao, Mongol, Norwegian, Polish, Portuguese, Punjabi, Romanian, Russian, Samoan, Serbo-Croatian, Slovak, Spanish, Swedish, Tai, Tajik, Thai, Turkish, Uighur, Ukrainian, Vietnamese, Yao, and Yiddish. The religions are Christian, Orthodox, Jewish, Muslim, Buddhist, Chinese folk-religion (a mixture of Confucianism and Taoism, which can still find followers in, besides China, many Chinese alien countries and regions), Hindu, Sikh, and Bahai. The population shares of the major linguistic and religious (or nonreligious) groups of the ten countries are listed in Table 3.2.[15]

We will estimate the model built in the previous section separately for the years 2000 (a year used to denote the post-Cold war period) and 1990 (a year used to denote the Cold war period). This enables us to check that the results are not artifact of any particular time period and to allow for changes in coefficients, especially on DISTANCE, LANGUAGE and RELIGION, that might have taken place due to changes in transportation and communication technology. In selecting the religions for measurement of RELIGION scores, such religions as 'folk religion' (but 'Chinese folk-religion' is an exception), 'traditional religion', 'atheism' and 'non-religion' were removed form Eq. (3.3). What we have done is due to the concern that these religions should not be scored as a common religion in the religious similarity measure. For example, 'traditional or folk religionists' from one nation (say, Togo) and 'traditional or folk religionists' form the other (say, China) do not have a common religious ground for people to trust each other.

Sources for the data on the dependent and explanatory variables in Eqs. (3.1) and (3.2) are as the following: (1) the International Monetary Fund (2003) for TRADE; (2) the World Bank (1991, 2001) and the United Nations (1986) for GNP

---

[14] See Appendix B. Of course, one can also include more countries. But this would increase the work of data processing significantly.

[15] In the Britannica Book (1996), atheism and non-religion were each treated as a 'religious affiliation' in USA and China, but in other countries such as Austria, Czech Republic, North Korea, etc., they were grouped as a single religious group.

Table 3.2 Shares of major linguistic groups and religious groups, by country (%)

linguistic groups, by country (%)

Country	Arabic		Chinese		English		French		German		Greek		Hindi		Italian	
	2000	1990	2000	1990	2000	1990	2000	1990	2000	1990	2000	1990	2000	1990	2000	1990
Brazil									0.55						0.42	
China			91.96	88.65												
Congo, Dem.							3.42									
France	2.53	2.63			0.14		93.68[a]	81.48		0.42					0.44	
India					3.58								50.22[b]	28.08		
Japan			0.17		0.06											
Saudi Arabia	95.02	97.00														
United States	0.14		0.51	0.29	87.53	88.99	0.74	0.73	0.61	0.73	0.15	0.18	0.13		0.51	0.74

Country	Japanese		Korean		Polish		Portuguese		Russian		Spanish		Turkish		Ukrainian	
	2000	1990	2000	1990	2000	1990	2000	1990	2000	1990	2000	1990	2000	1990	2000	1990
Brazil	0.38						97.55	98.97								
China			0.17	0.17												
Congo, Dem.																
France					0.09	0.64	1.14				0.38		0.34			
India																
Japan	99.09	99.43	0.53	0.47												
Saudi Arabia																
United States	0.17	0.15	0.25	0.12	0.28	0.37	0.17	0.17	0.09		6.78	5.33	0.02		0.04	

Table 3.2 continued

religious groups, by country (%)

Country	Christian		Orthodox		Jewish		Muslim		Buddhist		Hindu		Sikh		Bahai		Chinese folk religion	
	2000	1990	2000	1990	2000	1990	2000	1990	2000	1990	2000	1990	2000	1990	2000	1990	2000	1990
Brazil	95.49	93.90																
China	5.95						1.47	2.40	8.48	6.00							20.13	20.10
Congo, Dem.	85.99	77.43					1.39											
France	78.06	76.40			1.04		5.49	3.00										
India	3.51	2.64					11.05	11.20	0.72	0.70	80.26	82.70	1.96	1.90				
Japan	0.69	0.74							40.86	41.82								
Saudi Arabia							98.79	98.80										
United States	81.24	84.25	2.44	2.37	3.55	2.32	1.58		0.78		0.34		0.08		0.29			

Note Blanks denote that figures are less than 0.005

Source Calculated by the authors based on Britannica Book of the Year (1991 and 2001)

[a] Include naturalized citizens. Traditional dialects and minority languages are retained

[b] Include Hindi (lingua franca)

and GNPPC; and (3) calculation by the authors based on the World Atlas (1994) for DISTANCE and ADJACENT.

3.4 Empirical Evidence

Table 3.3 reports the estimated results of Eq. (3.1) for the years 1990 and 2000, respectively. The estimated coefficient on the natural log of DISTANCE is –1.163 for 1990 (statistically significant at the 1% confidence level) and –0.787 (statistically significant at the 1% confidence level) for 2000.[16] The reduction of geographical transactions costs might stem from many factors, one of which is the emergence of electronic commerce. While transactions are conducted via electronic devices, they may be transported using digital mechanisms, such as the download of a product from the Internet. It is the latter that provides the enabling mechanisms to foster the growth of electronic commerce. The actual and projected growth rates and uses of the Internet indicate that electronic commerce is no passing fad, but rather a fundamental change in the way in which businesses interact with one another and their consumers. The followings present the most obvious potential benefits from engaging in electronic commerce: (a) Internet and web-based electronic commerce can reach a more graphically dispersed customers base; (b) procurement processing costs can be lowered; (c) cost of purchasing can be lowered; (d) reductions in inventories; (e) lower cycle times; (f) better customer service; and (g) lower sales and, marketing costs (Greenstein and Feinman 2000, pp. 2–3).

The estimated coefficient on ADJACENT is statistically insignificant for international trade in both 1990 and 2000, showing that the eight countries did not have extraordinary trade growth with their neighboring countries and regions. This is perhaps because that, among the panel countries considered in this study, the U.S precisely had a common land border with only two countries (that is, Canada and Mexico) on the one hand, and that China and its neighboring countries either were separated by geographical barriers[17] or had not yet set up significant economic and trade relations (such as with Afghanistan and North Korea—two autarky economies) on the other hand. However, Table 3.3 does show a rising

---

[16] Among the past literature (see, for example, Linnemann 1966; Brada and Mendez 1983; Oguledo and MacPhee 1994; Bikker 1987; and Mansfield and Bronson 1997) relating to the determinants of international trade (in logarithmic form), the statistically significant coefficients on the log of distance have ranged between –0.51 and –1.50, which demonstrate the decreases (in percentage) in international trade as a result of a 1.0 percent increase in distance. Specifically, Linnemann (1966) estimates the coefficient as –0.77, Brada and Mendez (1983) and Oguledo and MacPhee (1994) as –0.76, Bikker (1987) as –0.90 to –1.1, and Mansfield and Bronson (1997) as –0.51 to –0.69 (for 1950–1990).

[17] Such as the mountains of Altai with Russia and Mongolia, Tian-Shan with Kazakhstan and Kyrgyzstan, and Himalayas with Bhutan, India and Nepal, and so on.

Table 3.3 The regressions for trade 1990 and 2000

Explanatory variable	Reg. (1)	Reg. (2)	Reg. (3)	Reg. (4)
The regressions for trade 1990				
(Constant)	−17.412 (2.241[a])	−18.156 (2.292[a])	−18.786 (2.326[a])	−19.152 (2.351[a])
$\ln(GNP_iGNP_j)$	1.067 (0.039[a])	1.068 (0.039[a])	1.075 (0.039[a])	1.075 (0.039[a])
$\ln(DISTANCE_{ij})$	−1.284 (0.168[a])	−1.217 (0.174[a])	−1.201 (0.172[a])	−1.163 (0.176[a])
$ADJACENT_{ij}$	0.673 (0.614)	0.760 (0.616)	0.643 (0.613)	0.708 (0.616)
$LANGUAGE_{ij}$		1.108 (0.721)		0.785 (0.741)
$RELIGION_{ij}$			0.750 (0.345[b])	0.662 (0.355[c])
Brazil	0.055 (0.396)	0.146 (0.401)	0.073 (0.396)	0.136 (0.400[a])
China	0.081 (0.395)	0.164 (0.398)	0.412 (0.423)	0.431 (0.423)
Congo (Dem.)	−2.601 (0.471[a])	−2.478 (0.478[a])	−2.491 (0.474[a])	−2.417 (0.479[a])
France	1.455 (0.400[a])	1.553 (0.405[a])	1.525 (0.400[a])	1.586 (0.405[a])
India	−1.167 (0.400[a])	−1.065 (0.405[a])	−0.855 (0.424[b])	−0.819 (0.426[b])
Japan	1.235 (0.384[a])	1.321 (0.387[a])	1.527 (0.406[a])	1.554 (0.407[a])
Saudi Arabia	−1.001 (0.423[b])	−0.966 (0.423[b])	−0.778 (0.434[c])	−0.779 (0.434[c])
R square	0.597	0.597	0.598	0.598
F-statistical value	186.5	169.9	170.4	156.3
Sig. of the regression	0.000	0.000	0.000	0.000
Number of observations	1296	1296	1296	1296
The regressions for trade 2000				
(Constant)	−23.984 (1.933[a])	−24.368 (1.954[a])	−24.298 (1.971[a])	−24.540 (1.982[a])
$\ln(GNP_iGNP_j)$	1.121 (0.035[a])	1.123 (0.035[a])	1.121 (0.035[a])	1.123 (0.035[a])
$\ln(DISTANCE_{ij})$	−0.825 (0.146[a])	−0.799 (0.148[a])	−0.802 (0.149[a])	−0.787 (0.150[a])
$ADJACENT_{ij}$	0.734 (0.498)	0.672 (0.500)	0.704 (0.500)	0.658 (0.501)
$LANGUAGE_{ij}$		0.805 (0.602)		0.732 (0.618)
$RELIGION_{ij}$			0.244 (0.300)	0.161 (0.308)
Brazil	−0.299 (0.340)	−0.219 (0.345)	−0.298 (0.340)	−0.226 (0.346)
China	0.657 (0.340[b])	0.740 (0.346[b])	0.754 (0.360[b])	0.796 (0.362[b])
Congo (Dem.)	−2.334 (0.387[a])	−2.231 (0.394[a])	−2.323 (0.387[a])	−2.233 (0.394[a])
France	0.634 (0.348[c])	0.689 (0.350[b])	0.650 (0.349[c])	0.694 (0.351[b])
India	0.202 (0.350)	0.293 (0.356)	0.292 (0.367)	0.344 (0.370)
Japan	−0.204 (0.330)	−0.120 (0.336)	−0.109 (0.350)	−0.0649 (0.352)
Saudi Arabia	−0.798 (0.371[b])	−0.740 (0.373[b])	−0.735 (0.379[b])	−0.704 (0.380[c])
R square	0.568	0.569	0.569	0.569
F-statistical value	203.9	185.6	185.4	170.1
Sig. of the regression	0.000	0.000	0.000	0.000
Number of observations	1568	1568	1568	1568

Note Figures within parentheses are standard errors

[a,b,c] Denote statistically significant at greater than the 1, 5 and 10% levels, respectively

trend in the contribution of ADJACENT to bilateral trade from 1990 to 2000, especially after taking ‘import’ into account. The estimated coefficient of

Fig. 3.2 The partial correlations between trade and cultural similarities

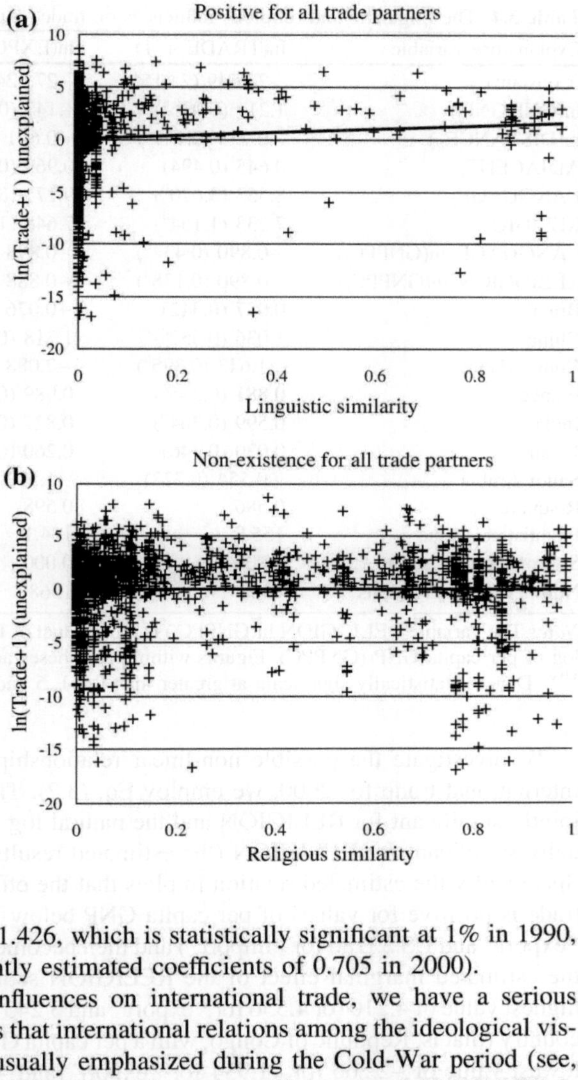

ADJACENT on 'import' is 1.426, which is statistically significant at 1% in 1990, compared to the insignificantly estimated coefficients of 0.705 in 2000).

Regarding the cultural influences on international trade, we have a serious concern about the hypothesis that international relations among the ideological vis-à-vis cultural friends were usually emphasized during the Cold-War period (see, for example, Huntington 1996). The estimated coefficient on LANGUAGE is statistically insignificant in both 1990 and 2000; it is, however, statistically insignificant for 'export' in both 1990 and 2000. These results show that from 1990 to 2000 'export' had been influenced by the linguistic factors more than 'import'. The estimated coefficient on RELIGION is significant in 1990 but not in 2000, which does not imply an increasing role of religious factors in international trade.

It seems that for the year 2000 the partial relation between ln(TRADE + 1) and LANGUAGE looks like a linear pattern (see Fig. 3.2a) but that between ln(TRADE + 1) and RELIGION does not (see Fig. 3.2b). Does this mean that international trade was no longer influenced by religious similarity in 2000?

Table 3.4 The linguistic and religious influences on trade, export and import, 2000

Explanatory variable	ln(TRADE + 1)	ln(EXPORT + 1)	ln(IMPORT + 1)
(Constant)	−28.549 (2.015[a])	−27.324 (1.976[a])	−35.440 (2.115[a])
$\ln(GNP_iGNP_j)$	1.217 (0.036[a])	1.147 (0.035[a])	1.385 (0.038[a])
$\ln(DISTANCE_{ij})$	−0.753 (0.147[a])	−0.691 (0.144[a])	−0.824 (0.154[a])
$ADJACENT_{ij}$	0.645 (0.494)	0.969 (0.484[b])	0.696 (0.518)
$LANGUAGE_{ij}$	8.553 (3.670[b])	9.171 (3.597[a])	7.176 (3.851[c])
$RELIGION_{ij}$	7.333 (1.154[a])	7.648 (1.131[a])	5.732 (1.211[a])
$LANGUAGE_{ij}\ln(GNPPC_j)$	−0.890 (0.434[b])	−0.898 (0.425[b])	−0.737 (0.455[c])
$RELIOGION_{ij}\ln(GNPPC_j)$	−0.890 (0.138[a])	−0.888 (0.135[a])	−0.712 (0.144[a])
Brazil	0.037 (0.342)	−0.076 (0.335)	−0.322 (0.358)
China	1.036 (0.357[a])	1.318 (0.350[a])	−0.203 (0.374)
Congo (Dem.)	−1.643 (0.395[a])	−2.088 (0.388[a])	−0.327 (0.415)
France	0.881 (0.345[a])	0.989 (0.338[a])	1.070 (0.362[a])
India	0.599 (0.364[b])	0.827 (0.357[b])	−0.152 (0.382)
Japan	0.030 (0.346)	0.260 (0.339)	−0.163 (0.363)
Saudi Arabia	−0.554 (0.373)	−1.592 (0.366[a])	−0.0164 (0.392)
R square	0.586	0.598	0.59
F-statistical value	155.8	164.1	161.1
Sig. of the regression	0.000	0.000	0.000
Number of observations	1568	1568	1568

Notes The variable RELIOGION $\ln(GNPPC_j)$ is the product of RELIGION scores and the natural log of per capita GNP (GNPPC). Figures within parentheses are standard errors
[a,b,c] Denote statistically significant at greater than the 1, 5 and 10% levels, respectively

To investigate the possible non-linear relationship between RFELIGION and international trade for 2000, we employ Eq. (3.2). The estimated coefficients are jointly significant for RELIGION and the natural log of GNPPC and also individually significant for RELIGION (the estimated results are reported in Table 3.4). Specifically the estimated relation implies that the effect of religious influence on trade is positive for values of per capita GNP below US $3767 (or US $5273 for "export" and US $3180 for "import") and then becomes negative.[18] Quantitatively, the estimated marginal effect of the RELIGION score on trade ranges from the highest value of 4.210 (or 4.536 for "export" and 3.245 for "import") for the poorest country (that is, Republic of Congo, with a per capita GNP of US $52 in 2000) to the lowest value of –2.266 (or –1.934 for "export" and –1.953 for "import") for the richest country (that is, Luxemburg, with a per capita GNP of US $37,785 in 2000).

As a check on these results, the trade model was re-estimated with the RELIGION scores allowed to have two separate coefficients. One coefficient applies for values of per capita GNP below US $3767 (or US $5273 for "export" and US $3180 for "import") (the break points estimated above) and other for values of per

[18] The three breakpoint values are obtained by letting the first-order differentials of the dependent variables ($\ln(TRADE_{ij} + 1)$, $\ln(EXPORT_{ij} + 1)$ and $\ln(IMPORT_{ij} + 1)$) with respect to RELIGION be zero, respectively.

Table 3.5 How religious influences on trade differ between low- and high-income partners, 2000

Explanatory variable	ln(TRADE + 1)	ln(EXPORT + 1)	ln(IMPORT + 1)
(Constant)	−26.974 (1.988[a])	−25.705 (1.938[a])	−34.208 (2.081[a])
$\ln(GNP_iGNP_j)$	1.185 (0.035[a])	1.108 (0.034[a])	1.360 (0.037[a])
$\ln(DISTANCE_{ij})$	−0.787 (0.147[a])	−0.704 (0.144[a])	−0.852 (0.154[a])
$ADJACENT_{ij}$	0.586 (0.494)	1.016 (0.483[b])	0.646 (0.518)
$LANGUAGE_{ij}$	1.112 (0.612[c])	1.775 (0.600[a])	1.017 (0.641)
$RELIGION_{ij}$ (high $GNPPC_j$)	−1.293 (0.373[a])	−1.323 (0.385[a])	−1.192 (0.391[a])
$RELIGION_{ij}$ (low $GNPPC_j$)	1.388 (0.355[a])	1.617 (0.334[a])	0.996 (0.372[a])
Brazil	−0.037 (0.342)	−0.077 (0.334)	−0.378 (0.358)
China	0.946 (0.358[a])	1.229 (0.350[a])	−0.273 (0.374)
Congo (Dem.)	−1.827 (0.394[a])	−2.293 (0.384[a])	−0.470 (0.412)
France	0.815 (0.346[a])	0.927 (0.339[a])	1.019 (0.362[a])
India	0.511 (0.365)	0.741 (0.357[b])	−0.221 (0.382)
Japan	−0.092 (0.348)	0.267 (0.340)	−0.172 (0.364)
Saudi Arabia	−0.592 (0.375)	−1.626 (0.366[a])	−0.193 (0.392)
R square	0.581	0.596	0.591
F-statistical value	165.0	175.3	172.0
Sig. of the regression	0.000	0.000	0.000
Number of observations	1568	1568	1568

Notes The system with RELIGION (low GNPPC) and RELIGION (high GNPPC) allows for two separate coefficients on the religion variable. The first coefficient applies when GNPPC is below the break point for a negative effect of RELIGION score on the dependent variable, as implied by the system that includes RELIGION and RELIGION*ln(GNPPC) in Table 3.4. The second coefficient applies for higher values of GNPPC. Figures within parentheses are standard errors
[a,b,c] Denote statistically significant at greater than the 1, 5 and 10% levels, respectively

capita GNP above them. The results, as shown in Table 3.5, are that the estimated coefficients of RELIGION on trade are 1.388 (or 1.617 for "export" and 0.896 for "import") in the low ranges of per capita GNP and –1.293 (or –1.323 for "export" and –1.192 for "import") in the high ranges. These estimated values are statistically significant at above 1% confidence level. Thus, this piecewise-linear form tells us a similar story to that found in the model that includes the interaction between the RELIGION and the natural log of per capita GNP in Table 3.4. Moreover, the absolute values of the above estimated coefficients show that, although import is slightly more sensitive to religious similarity with lower income partners than with higher income partners, 'export' is more sensitive to religious similarity with higher income partners than with lower income partners.

Figure 3.2 shows the partial relation between the log of TRADE and the RELIGION scores for the low and high ranges of per capita GNP. In Fig. 3.3a, where per capita GNP is below US $3767, the estimated relation is positive. In Fig. 3.3b, where per capita GNP is above US $3767, the estimated relation is negative. A possible interpretation of the above results involves the ideas that, although further evidence from both theoretical and empirical sides is still needed, the types of relation between cultural dissimilarity and comparative advantages of

Fig. 3.3 The partial correlations between trade and religious similarity

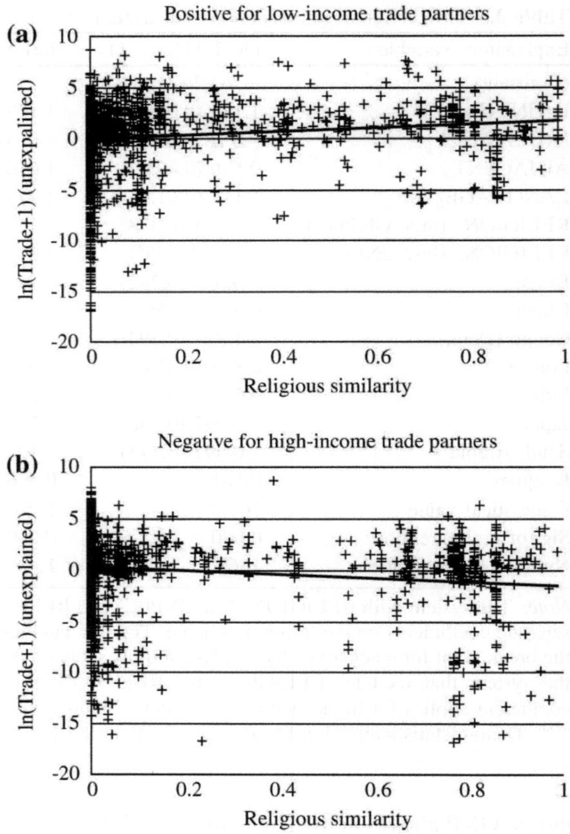

industrial production and consumption are determined by income level. Specifically, if other natural and geographical conditions are not considered, the comparative advantages can be found in culturally dissimilar economies more often than in culturally homogeneous places, the cost of intercultural transaction is usually higher in low-income nations (with low educational attainment and backward technological facilities) than in high-income nations (with high educational attainment and advanced technological facilities). At the meantime, the benefit from intercultural transaction in the high-income nations is usually higher or, at least not lower, than that in the low-income nations. This, as a result, tends to retard trade in poor economies and to encourage trade in richer places.

Economic determinants of trade seem controversial in existing studies. For example, according to the Heckscher-Ohlin theorem (see Heckscher 1919; and Ohlin 1933), countries with dissimilar levels of per capita income will trade more than countries with similar levels. However, a number of empirical results indicate that if the distribution of national incomes across countries becomes more equal over time, the volume of trade should increase.[19] Moreover, Helpman (1987) and Krugman (1995) predict that the sum of the logs of per capita GNPs of two countries will have a positive effect on the log form of trade between the two countries.

In order to present evidence to support trade dynamics with respect to income level, let us use again the estimated coefficients (as shown in Table 3.4). The first-order differentials of $\ln(\text{TRADE}_{ij} + 1)$, $\ln(\text{EXPORT}_{ij} + 1)$ and $\ln(\text{IMPORT}_{ij} + 1)$ with respect to $\ln\text{GNPPC}_j$ can be treated as the approximate measure of the elasticities of TRADE, EXPORT and IMPORT on per capita GNP, respectively, the sum of the estimated coefficients on $\ln(\text{GNP}_{ij}\text{GNP}_{ij})$ and RELIGION*ln(GNPPC_j) also imply approximately the elasticities of trade. As indicated by Table 3.4, the elasticities of TRADE, EXPORT and IMPORT with respect to GNPPC becomes "1.217−0.983*RELIGION", "1.147−0.982*RELIGION" and "1.385−0.789*RELIGION", respectively.[20] Obviously, while RELIGION ranges between 0 and 1, international trade of the eight countries selected in this research is always elastic to the income levels of their trade partners. In other words, for all the trade partners, increasing the level of per capita GNP will in any circumstances increase the international trade. In fact, if the estimated results based on panel data can be used to represent those of the rest of the world, they provide evidence that supports the views that international trade is more elastic to income level in religiously heterogeneous cultural countries and regions than in religiously homogeneous places.

At last, let us investigate how the cultural influences on trade differ from country to country. Following the regression model in Eq. (3.2), the effects of cultural influences on trade can be estimated using each of eight countries' panel data separately. For the year 2000, the estimated coefficients on LANGUAGE show that linguistic influence on trade is most significant in China, while it does not exist in Congo, Japan and Saudi Arabia (see Table 3.6). Particularly noteworthy is that France's foreign trade is negatively related to its linguistic similarity with respect to the trade partners.

We suspect that the stronger effect of linguistic influence on the Chinese foreign trade (especially on its export) might be attributable to the Chinese Diaspora, as ethnicity is more represented by linguistic than by religious identities. Rauch and Trindade (2002) also find that ethnic Chinese networks have a quantitatively important impact on bilateral trade through the mechanisms of market information and matching and referral services, in addition to their effect through community enforcement of sanctions that deter opportunistic behavior. Their estimated results show that for trade between countries with ethnic Chinese population shares at the

---

[19] For example, Linder (1961) predicts that countries with similar levels of per capita income will tend to have similar preferences with somewhat differentiated marketable goods, and thus will trade more with each other.

[20] Before deriving its first-order partial differential with respective to $\ln(\text{GNPPC}_j)$, the variable $\ln(\text{GNP}_i\text{GNP}_j)$ can be decomposed into $\ln(\text{POP}_i\text{POP}_j) + \ln(\text{GNPPC}_i) + \ln(\text{GNPPC}_j)$, where POP_i and POP_j are the sizes of population of the ith and jth countries, respectively.

Table 3.6 The estimated coefficients of cultural variables on foreign trade, by country, 2000

Country	Explanatory variable	ln(Trade + 1)	ln(Export + 1)	ln(Import + 1)
Brazil	$LANGUAGE_{ij}$	1.645 (1.686)	2.016 (1.594)	1.673 (1.967)
	$RELIGION_{ij}$	7.131 (2.184[a])	8.193 (2.065[a])	1.325 (2.548)
	$RELIOGION_{ij}ln(GNPPC_j)$	−1.041 (0.249[a])	−1.163 (0.235[a])	−0.316 (0.290)
China	$LANGUAGE_{ij}$	5.713 (1.785[a])	5.344 (1.685[a])	4.985 (2.342[b])
	$RELIGION_{ij}$	69.98 (14.83[a])	67.88 (14.00[a])	71.682 (19.45[a])
	$RELIOGION_{ij}ln(GNPPC_j)$	−9.292 (1.897[a])	−8.801 (1.791[a])	−9.465 (2.489[a])
Congo (Dem.)	$LANGUAGE_{ij}$	16.18 (19.98)	9.961 (17.766)	22.23 (19.48)
	$RELIGION_{ij}$	−0.364 (3.314)	−1.397 (2.946)	−1.790 (3.230)
	$RELIOGION_{ij}ln(GNPPC_j)$	0.099 (.384)	0.230 (.342)	0.222 (.375)
France	$LANGUAGE_{ij}$	−4.465 (1.320[a])	−3.846 (1.291[a])	−3.959 (1.254[a])
	$RELIGION_{ij}$	7.655 (2.823[a])	7.504 (2.762[a])	7.775 (2.682[a])
	$RELIOGION_{ij}ln(GNPPC_j)$	−0.932 (0.330[a])	−0.933 (0.323[a])	−0.877 (0.314[a])
India	$LANGUAGE_{ij}$	−0.522 (7.621)	1.366 (7.149)	−12.564 (8.614)
	$RELIGION_{ij}$	22.89 (9.60[a])	23.49 (9.00[a])	16.94 (1.85)
	$RELIOGION_{ij}ln(GNPPC_j)$	−2.303 (1.344[c])	−2.448 (1.261[b])	−1.198 (1.519)
Japan	$LANGUAGE_{ij}$	99.21 (282.92)	99.74 (269.31)	64.59 (28.75)
	$RELIGION_{ij}$	0.959 (9.654)	−0.274 (9.190)	5.623 (9.580)
	$RELIOGION_{ij}ln(GNPPC_j)$	−0.008 (1.327)	0.339 (1.263)	−0.807 (1.317)
Saudi Arabia	$LANGUAGE_{ij}$	1.142 (1.734)	2.218 (2.036)	1.496 (1.668)
	$RELIGION_{ij}$	6.564 (3.304)	6.772 (3.880[c])	5.012 (3.179[c])
	$RELIOGION_{ij}ln(GNPPC_j)$	−0.776 (0.502)	−0.516 (0.589)	−0.787 (0.483[c])
USA	$LANGUAGE_{ij}$	2.840 (1.075[a])	2.827 (1.031[a])	2.770 (1.129[b])
	$RELIGION_{ij}$	1.02 (2.67[a])	8.115 (2.558[a])	11.09 (2.80[a])
	$RELIOGION_{ij}ln(GNPPC_j)$	−1.209 (0.311[a])	−1.015 (0.299[a])	−1.200 (0.327[a])

Notes The number of observations is 198 for all countries' regressions. Only the estimated coefficients on cultural variables are listed in the table. Other regression statistics (F-statistic, R square, etc.) are omitted. Figures within parentheses are standard errors
[a,b,c] Denote statistical significant at the 1, 5 and 10% levels, respectively

levels prevailing in Southeast Asia, the smallest estimated average increase in bilateral trade in differentiated products attributable to ethnic Chinese networks is nearly 60%. But we still need more detailed evidence to explain why linguistic similarity it not helpful for the foreign trade between France and its trade partners.

The breakpoints of per capita GNP for a positive effect of the RELIGION on trade, as implied by the system that includes RELIGION and RELIGION*ln(GNPPC) in Table 3.6, are shown in Fig. 3.4. Specifically, the breakpoint values show that a positive effect of religious similarity on trade exists between Brazil and its partners with a per capita GNP of US $1000 or lower, between China and its partners with a per capita GNP of US $2000 or lower, and between both France and the U.S. and its partners with a per capita GNP of US $4000 or lower. However, the positive effect of religious similarity on trade only exists between India and its partners with a per capita GNP of US $21,000 or lower. Obviously, this indicates that religious retardation on foreign trade is much more significant in India than in Brazil and China.

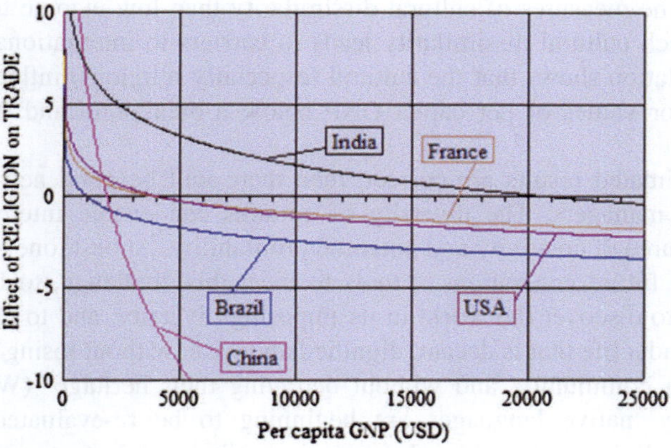

Fig. 3.4 The religious influences on trade, by country (*Source* derived from Table 3.6)

When considering export and import separately, we obtain similar results about the influences of religious similarity on foreign trade (see Table 3.6; Fig. 3.4).

3.5 Summary

Cultural influences on international trade are a complicated process. On the one hand, 'cultural dissimilarity' always generates the cost of intercultural transactions; on the other hand, it also results in 'economic complementarity', an important factor that has direct influences on trade. Although economists have attempted to quantitatively examine the effect of culture on international trade, few studies have dealt with the positive and negative correlations between the various cultural factors and trade.

We have clarified various economic conditions under which trade may be either encouraged or retarded. The adoption of a common standard between different cultural groups of people are not likely to be emphasized given that they have markedly differing attitudes as well as different cultural values. As a result, the larger the number of cultural groups involved in a multicultural society, *ceteris paribus*, the higher the managerial risks and costs resulting from it. However, in addition to the cost of intercultural transactions, 'cultural dissimilarity' may also generate more or less 'economic complementarities' that will have direct influences on trade.

Although there has had a growing concern about the role of culture in international trade, few studies have dealt quantitatively with the effects of the cultural influence. Using a gravity model on trade and the panel data of eight countries, we have found that cultural influences on international trade are more significant for the post-Cold War era than in the Cold War era. Our empirical results provide evidence supporting the presumption that high-income trade partners will be less sensitive to the measures of cultural dissimilarity than low-income trade partners between which cultural dissimilarity leads to barriers to international trade. This estimated relation shows that the cultural (especially religious) influence on trade is positive for values of per capita GNP below a breakpoint and then becomes negative.

If the estimated results are correct, then there will be good news for policy-makers and managers. The diversity of cultures can enable intercultural trade become a source of creativity and potential profitability. At best, one could provide 'present and future generations… tools to meet this challenge, to broaden their knowledge, to discover the world in its imposing diversity, and to allow all individuals to lead a life that is decent, dignified and wise, without losing their identity and sense of community, and without betraying their heritage' (WCCD 1995). Consequently, native languages are beginning to be re-evaluated, traditional knowledge rediscovered, and local economies revitalized. In fact, a world without the 'other' would be a world of stagnation, for, in culture as in nature, diversity holds the potential for innovation and creative, nonlinear solutions (Shanker 1996).

The treatment of linguistic and religious factors as continuous variables in this chapter has improved past studies in which 'language' was treated as one or more dummy variables and 'religion' was ignored. However, it should be noted that the data on linguistic and religious groups are not as accurate as those on the economic and geographical indicators used in this case study. Because of the difficulties encountered when quantifying linguistic and religious variables, only two years (1990 and 2000) were chosen to represent the Cold War era and the post-Cold War era, respectively. Obviously, more years of cross-sectional data are needed in order to provide more convincing comparisons between these two periods. This is especially true in East Asia, where many economies have experienced dramatic ideological and institutional transformations during the late 20th century. In future research, estimation of linguistic and religious influences on international trade should try to use more accurate linguistic and religious variables covering a longer period of time.

References

Baldwin RE (1971) Determinants of the commodity structure of US trade. Am Econ Rev 61:126–146

Bikker J (1987) An international trade flow model with substitution: an extension of the gravity model. Kyklos 40:315–337

Boisso D, Ferrantino M (1997) Economic distance, cultural distance and openness in international trade: empirical puzzles. J Econ Integration 12:456–484

Bowen HP, Leamer EE, Sveikauskas L (1987) Multicountry, multifactor tests of the factor abundance theory. Am Econ Rev 77(Dec):791–809

Brada J, Mendez J (1983) Regional economic integration and the volume of intra-regional trade: a comparison of developed and developing country experience. Kyklos 36:589–603

Branson WH, Monoyios N (1977) Factor inputs in US trade. J Int Econ 20:111–131

Britannica Book of the Year (various issues). Encyclopedia Britannica, Inc, Chicago

Deardorff A (1998) Determinants of bilateral trade: does gravity work in a classical world? In: Frankel JA (ed) The regionalization of the world economy. University of Chicago Press, Chicago, pp 213–243

Eichengreen B, Irwin D (1995) Trade blocs, currency blocs and the reorientation of trade in the 1930s. J Int Econ 38(2):89–106

Foroutan F, Pritchett L (1993) Intra-sub-Saharan African trade: is it too little? J African Econ 2(May):74–105

Frankel JA, Romer D (1996) Trade and growth. NBER working paper no. 5476. National Bureau of Economic Research, Cambridge

Frankel JA, Wei S-J (1995) European integration and the regionalization of world trade and currencies: the economics and the politics. In: Eichengreen B, Frieden F, von Hagen J (eds) Monetary and fiscal policy in an integrated Europe. Springer, New York, pp 89–123

Frankel JA, Romer D, Cyrus T (1995) Trade and growth in East Asian countries: cause and effect? Pacific Basin working paper series no. 95-03. Federal Reserve Bank of San Francisco, San Francisco

Frankel JA, Stein E, Wei S-J (1997a) Regional trading blocs in the world economic system. Institute for International Economics, Washington

Frankel JA, Stein E, Wei S-J (1997b) Trading blocs and the Americas: the natural, the unnatural, and the super-natural. J Dev Econ 47(1):61–95

Greenaway D, Milner CR (1986) The economics of intra-industry trade. Basil Blackwell, Oxford

Greenstein M, Feinman TM (2000) Electronic commerce: security, risk management. McGraw-Hill and China Machine Press, Beijing

Grossman G, Helpman E (1989) Product development and international trade. J Political Econ 97:1261–1283

Grossman G, Helpman E (1991) Innovation and growth in the world economy. The MIT Press, Cambridge

Grubel HG, Lloyd PJ (1975) Intra-industry trade: the theory and measurement of international trade in differentiated products. Macmillan Press, London

Guo R (2004) How culture influences foreign trade—evidence from the US and China. J Socio-Econ 33(6):785–812

Guo R (2006) Cultural influences on economic analysis—theory and empirical evidence. Palgrave-Macmillan, New York

Havrylyshyn O, Pritchett L (1991) European trade patterns after the transition. Policy, research and external affairs working paper series no. 74. World Bank, Washington

Heckscher EF (1919) The effect of foreign trade on the distribution of income. Ekonomisk Tidskirift 21:497–512. Reprinted in Ellis HS, Metzler LM (eds) (1950) Readings in the theory of international trade. Irwin, Homewood, pp 272–300

Helpman E (1987) Imperfect competition and international trade: evidence from fourteen industrial countries. J Jpn Int Econ 1:62–81

Huntington SP (1996) The clash of civilization and the remaking of world order. Simon & Schuster, New York

International Monetary Fund (various issues) Direction of Trade Statistics. Washington: the IMF

Isard W (1949) Gravity, potential, and spatial interaction models. Reprinted in Smith C (ed) (1990) Practical methods of regional science and empirical applications: selected papers of Walter Isard, vol 2. New York University Press, New Work, pp 1–23

Keesing DB (1966) Labor skills and comparative advantage. Am Econ Rev 56:249–258

Kenen P (1965) Nature, capital and trade. J Political Econ 73:437–460

Kravis IB (1956a) Wages and foreign trade. Rev Econ Stat 38:14–30

Kravis IB (1956b) Availability and other influences on the commodity composition of trade. J Political Econ 73:143–155

Krugman PR (1980) Scale economies, product differentiation, and the pattern of trade. Am Econ Rev 70:950–959

Krugman PR (1995) Growing world trade: causes and consequences. Brook Pap Econ Act 1:327–362

Lancaster K (1980) Intra-industry trade under perfect monopolistic competition. J Int Econ 23:151–175
Leamer EE (1980) The Leontef Paradox reconsidered. J Political Econ 88(June):495–503
Leamer EE (1984) Sources for international comparative advantage. The MIT Press, Cambridge
Leamer EE (1993) Factor-supply differences as a source of comparative advantage. Am Econ Rev 83(May):436–444
Leontief W (1954) Domestic production and foreign trade: the American capital position re-examined. Econ Int 7:2–32. Reprinted in Bhagwati JH (ed) (1969) International trade: selected readings. Penguin, Baltimore, pp 3–16
Leontief W (1956) Factor proportions and the structure of American trade; further theoretical and empirical analysis. Rev Econ Stat 38:386–407
Linder SB (1961) An essay on trade and transformation. Wiley, New York
Linnemann H (1966) An econometric study of international trade theory. North-Holland, Amsterdam
Mansfield E, Bronson R (1997) The political economy of major-power trade flows. In: Mansfield E, Milner H (eds) The political economy of regionalism. Columbia University Press, New York, pp 213–256
Markusen J (1986) Explaining the volume of trade: an eclectic approach. Am Econ Rev 76:1002–1011
Noland M (2005) Affinity and international trade. Institute for international economics, Washington DC, Working paper series no. WP 05-3, June
Oguledo V, MacPhee C (1994) Gravity models: a reformulation and an application to discriminatory trade arrangement. Appl Econ 26:107–120
Ohlin B (1933) Interregional and international trade. Harvard University Press, Cambridge
Pöyhönen P (1963) A tentative model for the volume of trade between countries. Weltwirtschaftliches Archiv 90(1):93–99
Rauch JE (1999) Networks versus markets in international trade. J Int Econ 48:7–35
Rauch JE, Trindade V (2002) Ethnic Chinese networks in international trade. Rev Econ Stat 84(1):116–130
Rivera-Batiz L, Romer P (1991) International trade and endogenous growth. Q J Econ 106:531–555
Rose A (2004) Do we really know that the WTO increases trade? Am Econ Rev 94:98–114
Salvatore D (1995) International economics, 5th edn. Prentice-Hall International, Inc, New York
Salvatore D, Barazesh R (1990) The factor content of US foreign trade and the Heckscher-Ohlin theory. Int Trade J 16(winter):149–181
Samuelson PA (1948) International trade and the equalization of factor prices. Econ J 58(June):165–184
Samuelson PA (1949) International factor-price equalization once again. Econ J 59:181–197. Reprinted in Bhagwati JN (ed) (1981) International trade: selected readings. The MIT Press, Cambridge, pp 93–139
Shanker R (1996) Culture and development. Development express, no. 8. International Development Information Center, Hull
Stern RM, Maskus KE (1981) Determinants of the structure of US Foreign trade. J Int Econ 24:207–224
Stewart JQ (1948) Demographic gravitation: evidence and applications. Sociometry 2:31–58
Tinbergen J (1962) An analysis of world trade flows, the Linder hypothesis, and exchange risk. In: Tinbergen J (ed) Shaping the world economy. The Twentieth Century Fund, New York, pp 20–42
United Nations (1986) Annual statistical yearbook. UN, New York
Vona S (1990) Intra-industry trade: a statistical prefect or a real phenomenon? Banca Naz. Lavoro Q Rev, December, 487–497
Wilson EA (1980) Sociobiology. Belknap, Cambridge
World Atlas (1994) Rand McNally & Company, USA, 1994
World Bank (1991) World Bank Atlas. The World Bank, Washington

World Bank (2001) World development indicators. The World Bank, Washington
World Commission on Culture and Development (WCCD) (1995) Our creative diversity. United Nations's Science, Education and Culture Organization (UNSECO), Paris
Zipf GK (1946) The P^1P^2/D hypothesis: on the intercity movement of persons. Am Sociol Rev 11(6):677–686

Appendix A
Cultural Characteristics of the World

Economy	Major ethnic groups	Major linguistic groups	Major religious groups
Afghanistan	Pashtun, Tajik, Hazara, Uzbek, Aimak, Turkmen, Baloch	Afghan Persian (Dari), Pashtu, Uzbek, Turkmen, Balochi, Pashai	Sunni Muslim, Shi'a Muslim
Albania	Albanian, Greek, Vlach, Roma (Gypsy), Serb, Macedonian, Bulgarian	Albanian, Greek, Vlach, Romani, Slavic dialects	Muslim, Albanian Orthodox, Roman Catholic
Algeria	Arab-Berber, European	Arabic, French, Berber dialects	Sunni Muslim (state religion), Christian, Jewish
American Samoa	Native Pacific islander, Asian, white, mixed	Samoan, English, Tongan, other Pacific islander	Christian Congregationalist, Roman Catholic, Protestant
Andorra	Spanish, Andorran, Portuguese, French	Catalan, French, Castilian, Portuguese	Roman Catholic
Angola	Ovimbundu, Kimbundu, Bakongo, mixed European and African, European	Portuguese, Bantu and other African languages	Indigenous beliefs, Roman Catholic, Protestant
Anguilla	Black, mixed, mulatto, white	English	Anglican, Methodist, other Protestant, Roman Catholic, other Christian
Antigua and Barbuda	Black, British, Portuguese, Lebanese, Syrian	English, local dialects	Christian (predominantly Anglican with other Protestant, and some Roman Catholic)
Argentina	White (mostly Spanish and Italian), mixed white and Amerindian ancestry, Amerindian	Spanish, English, Italian, German, French	Roman Catholic, Protestant, Jewish

(continued)

R. Guo, *Introduction to Intercultural Economics*, SpringerBriefs in Economics,
DOI: 10.1007/978-3-642-29276-7, © The Author(s) 2012

(continued)

Economy	Major ethnic groups	Major linguistic groups	Major religious groups
Armenia	Armenian, Yezidi (Kurd), Russian	Armenian, Yezidi, Russian	Armenian Apostolic, other Christian, Yezidi (monotheist with elements of nature worship)
Aruba	Mixed white/Caribbean Amerindian	Dutch, Papiamento (a Spanish, Portuguese, Dutch, English dialect), English, Spanish	Roman Catholic, Protestant, Hindu, Muslim, Confucian, Jewish
Australia	Caucasian, Asian, aboriginal	English, Chinese, Italian	Catholic, Anglican, other Christian, Buddhist, Muslim
Austria	Austrians, Croatians, Slovenes, Serbs, and Bosniaks, Turks, German	German, Slovene, Croatian, Hungarian	Roman Catholic, Protestant, Muslim
Azerbaijan	Azeri, Dagestani, Russian, Armenian	Azerbaijani (Azeri), Russian, Armenian	Muslim, Russian Orthodox, Armenian Orthodox
Bahamas, The	Black, white, Asian and Hispanic	English, Creole	Baptist, Anglican, Roman Catholic, Pentecostal, Church of God, Methodist, other Christian
Bahrain	Bahraini, non-Bahraini	Arabic, English, Farsi, Urdu	Muslim (Shi'a and Sunni), Christian
Bangladesh	Bengali, tribal groups, non-Bengali Muslims	Bangla (Bengali), English	Muslim, Hindu
Barbados	Black, white, Asian and mixed	English	Anglican, Pentecostal, Methodist, other Protestant, Roman Catholic
Belarus	Belarusian, Russian, Polish, Ukrainian	Belarusian, Russian	Eastern Orthodox, Roman Catholic, Protestant, Jewish, and Muslim
Belgium	Fleming, Walloon, mixed	Dutch, French, German	Roman Catholic, Protestant
Belize	Mestizo, Creole, Maya, Garifuna	English, Spanish, Mayan, Garifuna (Carib), Creole	Roman Catholic, Protestant
Benin	Fon, Adja, Yoruba, Bariba, etc, Europeans	French, Fon and Yoruba (in south), tribal languages	Indigenous beliefs, Christian, Muslim
Bermuda	Black, white, mixed, other races	English, Portuguese	Anglican, Roman Catholic, African Methodist Episcopal, other Protestant

(continued)

(continued)

Economy	Major ethnic groups	Major linguistic groups	Major religious groups
Bhutan	Bhote, Ethnic Nepalese, Indigenous or Migrant tribes	Dzongkha, Tibetan dialects, Nepalese dialects	Lamaistic Buddhist, Hinduism
Bolivia	Quechua, mixed white and Amerindian ancestry, Aymara, white	Spanish, Quechua, Aymara	Roman Catholic, Protestant (Evangelical Methodist)
Bosnia and	Herzegovina	Bosniak, Serb, Croat	Bosnian, Croatian, Serbian
Muslim, Orthodox, Roman Catholic			
Botswana	Tswana (or Setswana), Kalanga, Basarwa, Kgalagadi	Setswana, Kalanga, Sekgalagadi, English	Christian, Badimo
Brazil	White, mulatto, black, Japanese, Arab, and Amerindian	Portuguese, Spanish, English, French	Roman Catholic, Protestant, Spiritualist, Bantu/ voodoo
British Virgin Islands	Black, white, Indian, Asian and mixed	English	Protestant, Roman Catholic
Brunei	Malay, Chinese, Indigenous	Bahasa-Malay, English, Chinese	Muslim, Buddhist, Christian, indigenous beliefs
Bulgaria	Bulgarian, Turk, Roma, Macedonian, Armenian, Tatar, and Circassian	Bulgarian, Turkish, Roma	Bulgarian Orthodox, Muslim, other Christian
Burkina Faso	Mossi over, Gurunsi, Senufo, Lobi, Bobo, Mande, Fulani	French, Native African languages	Muslim, indigenous beliefs, Roman Catholic
Burma (Myanmar)	Burmese, minority ethnic languages	Buddhist, Christian, Muslim, animist	Burman, Shan, Karen, Rakhine, Chinese, Indian, Mon
Burundi	Hutu (Bantu), Tutsi (Hamitic), Twa (Pygmy), Europeans, South Asians	Kirundi, French, Swahili (along Lake Tanganyika and in the Bujumbura area)	Roman Catholic, Indigenous beliefs, Muslim, Protestant
Cambodia	Khmer, Vietnamese, Chinese, other	Khmer, French, English	Theravada Buddhist
Cameroon	Cameroon Highlanders, Equatorial/ Northwestern Bantu, Kirdi, Fulani, Eastern Nigritic	Major African language groups, English, French	Indigenous beliefs, Christian, Muslim

(continued)

(continued)

Economy	Major ethnic groups	Major linguistic groups	Major religious groups
Canada	British Isles origin, French origin, other European, Amerindian, Asian, African, and Arab	English, French	Roman Catholic, Protestant, other Christian, Muslim
Cape Verde	Creole (mulatto), African, European	Portuguese, Crioulo (a blend of Portuguese and West African words)	Roman Catholic (infused with indigenous beliefs); Protestant (mostly Church of the Nazarene)
Cayman Islands	Mixed, white, black, expatriates of various ethnic groups	English	United Church, Anglican, Baptist, Church of God, other Protestant, Roman Catholic
Central African Republic	Baya, Banda, Mandjia, Sara, Mboum, M'Baka, Yakoma	French, Sangho (lingua franca), tribal languages	Indigenous beliefs, Protestant, Roman Catholic, Muslim
Chad	Arabs, Gorane, Zaghawa, Kanembou, Ouaddai, Baguirmi, Hadjerai, Fulbe, Kotoko, Hausa, Boulala, and Maba (in north and center); Sara, Moundang, Moussei, Massa (in south)	French, Arabic, Sara (in south), over other languages and dialects	Muslim, Christian, animist
Chile	White and white-Amerindian, Amerindian	Spanish	Roman Catholic, Protestant, Jewish
China	Han Chinese, Zhuang, Uygur, Hui, Yi, Tibetan, Miao, Manchu, Mongol, Buyi, Korean	Mandarin, Cantonese, Wu, Minnan (Taiwanese), Xiang, Gan, Hakka dialects	Chinese-folk religion, Buddhist, Christian, Muslim
Christmas Island	Chinese, European, Malay	English, Chinese, Bahasa-Malay	Buddhist, Muslim, Christian
Cocos (Keeling) Islands	Europeans, Cocos Malays	Bahasa-Malay (Cocos dialect), English	Sunni Muslim
Colombia	Mestizo, White, Mulatto, Black, Mixed black-Amerindian, Amerindian	Spanish	Roman Catholic
Comoros	Antalote, Cafre, Makoa, Oimatsaha, Sakalava	Arabic, French, Shikomoro (a blend of Swahili and Arabic)	Sunni Muslim, Roman Catholic

(continued)

(continued)

Economy	Major ethnic groups	Major linguistic groups	Major religious groups
Congo,	Democratic Republic of the	Mongo, Luba, Kongo (all Bantu), Mangbetu-Azande (Hamitic)	French, Lingala (lingua franca), Kingwana (dialect of Kiswahili or Swahili), Kikongo, Tshiluba
Roman Catholic, Protestant,	Kimbanguist, Muslim		
Congo, Republic of the	Kongo, Sangha, M'Bochi, Teke, Europeans	French, Lingala and Monokutuba (lingua franca), Kikongo	Christian, animist, Muslim
Cook Islands	Cook Island Maori (Polynesian), part Cook Island Maori	English, Maori	Cook Islands Christian Church, Roman Catholic, Seventh-Day Adventists, Church of Latter Day Saints, other Protestant
Costa Rica	White (including mestizo), Black, Amerindian, Chinese	Spanish, English	Roman Catholic, Evangelical, Jehovah's Witnesses, other Protestant
Cote d'Ivoire	Akan, Voltaiques or Gur, Northern Mandes, Krous, Southern Mandes	French, native dialects with Dioula the most widely spoken	Muslim, Indigenous, Christian
Croatia	Croat, Serb, Bosniak, Hungarian, Slovene, Czech, Roma	Croatian, Serbian, Italian, Hungarian, Czech, Slovak, and German	Roman Catholic, Orthodox, other Christian, Muslim
Cuba	Mulatto, White, Black, Chinese	Spanish	Roman Catholic, Protestants, Jehovah's Witnesses, Jews, and Santeria
Cyprus	Greek, Turkish	Greek, Turkish, English	Greek Orthodox, Muslim, Maronite, Armenian Apostolic
Czech Republic	Czech, Moravian, Slovak	Czech	Roman Catholic, Protestant
Denmark	Scandinavian, Inuit, Faroese, German, Turkish, Iranian, Somali	Danish, Faroese, Greenlandic (an Inuit dialect), German	Evangelical Lutheran, other Protestant and Roman Catholic, Muslim
Djibouti	Somali, Afar, French, Arab, Ethiopian, and Italian	French, Arabic, Somali, Afar	Muslim, Christian
Dominica	Black, Mixed Black and European, European, Syrian, Carib Amerindian	English, French patois	Roman Catholic, Protestant

(continued)

(continued)

Economy	Major ethnic groups	Major linguistic groups	Major religious groups
Dominican Republic	mixed, white, black	Spanish	Roman Catholic
East Timor	Austronesian (Malayo-Polynesian), Papuan, small Chinese minority	Tetum, Portuguese, Indonesian, English	Roman Catholic, Muslim, Protestant, Hindu, Buddhist, Animist
Ecuador	mestizo (mixed Amerindian and white), Amerindian, Spanish, black	Spanish, Amerindian languages (especially Quechua)	Roman Catholic
Egypt	Egyptian, Berber, Nubian, Bedouin, and Beja, Greek, Armenian, other Europeans	Arabic, English and French	Muslim (mostly Sunni), Coptic, other Christian
El Salvador	Mestizo, white, Amerindian	Spanish, Nahua (among some Amerindians)	Roman Catholic, other
Equatorial Guinea	Bioko (primarily Bubi, some Fernandinos), Rio Muni (primarily Fang), Spanish	Spanish, French, pidgin English, Fang, Bubi, Ibo	Christian (predominantly Roman Catholic), pagan practices
Eritrea	ethnic Tigrinya, Tigre and Kunama, Afar, Saho (Red Sea coast dwellers)	Afar, Arabic, Tigre and Kunama, Tigrinya, other Cushitic languages	Muslim, Coptic Christian, Roman Catholic, Protestant
Estonia	Estonian, Russian, Ukrainian, Belarusian, Finn	Estonian, Russian	Evangelical Lutheran, Orthodox, other Christian
Ethiopia	Oromo, Amhara and Tigre, Sidamo, Shankella, Somali, Afar, Gurage	Amharic, Tigrinya, Oromigna, Guaragigna, Somali, Arabic, English	Muslim, Ethiopian Orthodox, animist
Fiji	Fijian (predominantly Melanesian with a Polynesian admixture), Indian, European, other Pacific Islanders, Chinese	English, Fijian, Hindustani	Christian, Hindu, Muslim
Finland	Finn, Swede, Russian, Estonian, Roma, Sami	Finnish, Swedish, Sami and Russian	Lutheran National Church, Greek Orthodox in Finland, other Christian
France	Celtic and Latin with Teutonic, Slavic, North African, Indochinese, Basque minorities	French, Provencal, Breton, Alsatian, Corsican, Catalan, Basque, Flemish	Roman Catholic, Muslim, Protestant, Jewish

(continued)

(continued)

Economy	Major ethnic groups	Major linguistic groups	Major religious groups
French Guiana	Black or Mulatto, White, East Indian, Chinese, Amerindian	French	Roman Catholic
French Polynesia	Polynesian, Chinese, local French, metropolitan French	French, Polynesian, Asian languages	Protestant, Roman Catholic
Gabon	Bantu tribes (including Fang, Bapounou, Nzebi, Obamba), other Africans and Europeans	French, Fang, Myene, Nzebi, Bapounou/Eschira, Bandjabi	Christian, animist, Muslim
Gambia, The	Mandinka, Fula, Wolof, Jola, Serahuli, non-African	English, Mandinka, Wolof, Fula, other indigenous vernaculars	Muslim, Christian, indigenous beliefs
Gaza Strip	Palestinian Arab, Jewish	Arabic, Hebrew (spoken by many Palestinians), English	Muslim (predominantly Sunni), Christian, Jewish
Georgia	Georgian, Azeri, Armenian, Russian	Georgian, Russian, Armenian, Azeri	Orthodox Christian, Muslim, Armenian-Gregorian, Catholic
Germany	German, Turkish, Greek, Italian, Polish, Russian, Serbo-Croatian, Spanish	German	Protestant, Roman Catholic, Muslim
Ghana	Akan, Moshi-Dagomba, Ewe, Ga, Gurma, Yoruba, European	English, Akan, Moshi-Dagomba, Ewe, Ga	Christian, Muslim, Indigenous beliefs
Gibraltar	Spanish, Italian, English, Maltese, Portuguese, German, North Africans	English, Spanish, Italian, Portuguese	Roman Catholic, Church of England, other Christian, Muslim, Jewish, Hindu
Greece	Greek, other	Greek, English, French	Greek Orthodox, Muslim
Greenland	Greenlander (Inuit and Greenland-born whites), Danish	Greenlandic (East Inuit), Danish, English	Evangelical Lutheran
Grenada	Black, Mixed Black and European, European and East Indian, and trace of Arawak/Carib Amerindian	English, French patois	Roman Catholic, Anglican, other Protestant
Guadeloupe	Black or Mulatto, White, East Indian, Lebanese, Chinese	French, Creole Patois	Roman Catholic, Hindu and Pagan African, Protestant
Guam	Chamorro, Filipino, other Pacific islander, white, other Asian	English, Chamorro, Philippine languages, other Pacific island languages, Asian languages	Roman Catholic

(continued)

(continued)

Economy	Major ethnic groups	Major linguistic groups	Major religious groups
Guatemala	Mestizo and European, K'iche, Kaqchikel, Mam, Q'eqchi, other Mayan, non-Mayan	Spanish, Amerindian languages	Roman Catholic, Protestant, Indigenous Mayan beliefs
Guernsey	UK and Norman-French descent with small percentages from other European countries	English, French, Norman-French dialect	Anglican, Roman Catholic, Presbyterian, Baptist, Congregational, Methodist
Guinea	Peuhl, Malinke, Soussou, smaller ethnic groups	French	Muslim, Christian, Indigenous beliefs
Guinea-Bissau	Balanta, Fula, Manjaca, Mandinga, Papel, European and mulatto	Portuguese, Crioulo, African languages	Indigenous beliefs, Muslim, Christian
Guyana	East Indian, black, Amerindian, white, Chinese, mixed	English, Amerindian dialects, Creole, Hindi, Urdu	Christian, Hindu, Muslim
Haiti	Black, Mulatto, White	French, Creole	Roman Catholic, Baptist, Pentecostal, Adventist
Honduras	Mestizo (mixed Amerindian and European), Amerindian, black, white	Spanish, Amerindian dialects	Roman Catholic, Protestant
Hong Kong	Chinese, other	Chinese (Cantonese), English	Eclectic mixture of local Religions, Christian
Hungary	Hungarian, Roma, other or unknown	Hungarian, other or unspecified	Roman Catholic, Calvinist, Lutheran, Greek Catholic, other Christian
Iceland	mix of descendants of Norse and Celts, population of foreign origin	Icelandic, English, Nordic languages, German	Lutheran Church of Iceland, Roman Catholic, Free Church (Reykjavik/ Hafnarfjorour), other Christian
India	Indo-Aryan, Dravidian, Mongoloid	English, Hindi, Bengali, Telugu, Marathi, Tamil, Urdu, Gujarati, Malayalam, Kannada, Oriya, Punjabi, Assamese, Kashmiri, Sindhi, and Sanskrit	Hindu, Muslim, Christian, Sikh
Indonesia	Javanese, Sundanese, Madurese, coastal Malays	Bahasa Indonesia, English, Dutch, local dialects (of which Javanese is most widely spoken)	Muslim, Protestant, Roman Catholic, Hindu, Buddhist

(continued)

(continued)

Economy	Major ethnic groups	Major linguistic groups	Major religious groups
Iran	Persian, Azeri, Gilaki and Mazandarani, Kurd, Arab, Lur, Baloch, Turkmen	Persian and Persian dialects, Turkic and Turkic dialects, Kurdish, Luri, Balochi, Arabic, Turkish	Shi'a Muslim, Sunni Muslim, Zoroastrian, Jewish, Christian, and Baha'I
Iraq	Arab, Kurdish, Turkoman, Assyrian	Arabic, Kurdish, Assyrian, Armenian	Muslim (Shi'a, Sunni), Christian
Ireland	Celtic, English	English, Irish, Gaelic (or Gaeilge)	Roman Catholic, Church of Ireland, other Christian
Isle of Man	Manx (Norse-Celtic descent), Briton	English, Manx Gaelic	Anglican, Roman Catholic, Methodist, Baptist, Presbyterian, Society of Friends
Israel	Jewish, Arab	Hebrew, Arabic, English	Jewish, Muslim, Arab Christians, other Christian, Druze
Italy	Italian, small clusters of German, French, and Slovene-Italians in north, Albanian-Italians and Greek-Italians in south	Italian, German, French, Slovene	Roman Catholic ; Protestant, Jewish, Muslim
Jamaica	Black, East Indian, White, Chinese, Mixed	English, patois English	Protestant, Roman Catholic
Japan	Japanese, Korean, Chinese, Brazilian, Filipino	Japanese	Both Shinto and Buddhist, Christian
Jersey	Jersey, British, Irish, French, and other white, Portuguese/ Madeiran	English, Portuguese	Anglican, Roman Catholic, Baptist, Congregational New Church, Methodist, Presbyterian
Jordan	Arab, Circassian, Armenian	Arabic, English	Sunni Muslim, Christian, Shi'a Muslim
Kazakhstan	Kazakh (Qazaq), Russian, Ukrainian, Uzbek, German, Tatar, Uygur	Kazakh (Qazaq, state language), Russian	Muslim, Russian Orthodox, Protestant
Kenya	Kikuyu, Luhya, Luo, Kalenjin, Kamba, Kisii, Meru, Asian, European, Arab	English, Kiswahili, numerous indigenous languages	Protestant, Roman Catholic, indigenous beliefs, Muslim

(continued)

(continued)

Economy	Major ethnic groups	Major linguistic groups	Major religious groups
Kiribati	Micronesian	I-Kiribati, English	Roman Catholic, Protestant (Congregational), some Seventh-Day Adventist, Muslim, Baha'i, Latter-day Saints, Church of God
Korea, North	Korean, Chinese, ethnic Japanese	Korean	Buddhist, Confucianist, Christian, Chondogyo
Korea, South	Korean, Chinese	Korean, English	Christian, Buddhist, Confucianist, Chondogyo
Kuwait	Kuwaiti, other Arab, South Asian, Iranian	Arabic, English	Muslim (Sunni, Shi'a), Christian, Hindu, Parsi
Kyrgyzstan	Kyrgyz, Uzbek, Russian, Dungan, Ukrainian, Uygur	Kyrgyz, Russian	Muslim, Russian Orthodox
Laos	Lao Loum (lowland), Lao Theung (upland), Lao Soung (highland), Vietnamese, Chinese	Lao, French, English, and various ethnic languages	Buddhist, animist, Christian
Latvia	Latvian, Russian, Belarusian, Ukrainian, Polish, Lithuanian	Latvian, Russian, Lithuanian	Lutheran, Roman Catholic, Russian Orthodox
Lebanon	Arab, Armenian, other	Arabic, French, English, Armenian	Muslim (Shi'a, Sunni, Druze, etc.), Catholic, Orthodox, Protestant
Lesotho	Sotho, Europeans, Asians	Sesotho (southern Sotho), English, Zulu, Xhosa	Christian, indigenous beliefs
Liberia	Kpelle, Bassa, Gio, Kru, Grebo, Mano, Krahn, Gola, Gbandi, Loma, Kissi, Vai, Dei, Bella, Mandingo, and Mende, Americo-Liberians, Congo People	English, some ethnic group languages	indigenous beliefs, Christian, Muslim
Libya	Berber and Arab, Greeks, Maltese, Italians, Egyptians, Pakistanis, Turks, Indians, Tunisians	Arabic, Italian, English	Sunni Muslim
Liechtenstein	Alemannic, Italian, Turkish	German, Alemannic dialect	Roman Catholic, Protestant
Lithuania	Lithuanian, Polish, Russian	Lithuanian, Russian, Polish	Roman Catholic, Russian Orthodox, Protestant

(continued)

(continued)

Economy	Major ethnic groups	Major linguistic groups	Major religious groups
Luxembourg	Celtic base (with French and German blend), Portuguese, Italian, Slavs, European	Luxembourgish (national language), German (administrative language), French (administrative language)	Roman Catholic, Protestants, Jews, and Muslims
Macau	Chinese, Macanese (mixed Portuguese and Asian ancestry)	Cantonese, Hokkien, Mandarin, other Chinese dialects	Buddhist, Roman Catholic
Macedonia	Macedonian, Albanian, Turkish, Roma, Serb	Macedonian, Albanian, Turkish, Roma, Serbian	Macedonian Orthodox, Muslim, other Christian
Madagascar	Malayo-Indonesian, Cotiers (mixed African, Malayo-Indonesian, and Arab ancestry), French, Indian, Creole, Comoran	French, Malagasy	Indigenous beliefs, Christian, Muslim
Malawi	Chewa, Nyanja, Tumbuka, Yao, Lomwe, Sena, Tonga, Ngoni, Ngonde, Asian, European	Chichewa, Chinyanja, Chiyao, Chitumbuka, Chisena, Chilomwe, Chitonga	Christian, Muslim
Malaysia	Malay, Chinese, Indigenous, Indian	Bahasa Melayu, English, Chinese, Tamil, Telugu, Malayalam, Panjabi, Thai	Muslim, Buddhist, Daoist, Hindu, Christian, Sikh, Shamanism
Maldives	South Indians, Sinhalese, Arabs	Maldivian Dhivehi (dialect of Sinhala, script derived from Arabic), English	Sunni Muslim
Mali	Mande, Peul, Voltaic, Songhai, Tuareg, Moor	French, Bambara, numerous African languages	Muslim, Indigenous beliefs, Christian
Malta	Maltese (with elements of Italian and other Mediterranean stock)	Maltese, English	Roman Catholic
Marshall Islands	Micronesian	Marshallese, other languages	Protestant, Assembly of God, Roman Catholic, Bukot nan Jesus, Mormon, other Christian
Martinique	African and African-white-Indian mixture, white, East Indian, Chinese	French, Creole patois	Roman Catholic, Protestant, Muslim, Hindu
Mauritania	mixed Maur/black, Moor, black	Arabic, Pulaar, Soninke, French, Hassaniya, Wolof	Muslim

(continued)

(continued)

Economy	Major ethnic groups	Major linguistic groups	Major religious groups
Mauritius	Indo-Mauritian, Creole, Sino-Mauritian, Franco-Mauritian	Creole, Bhojpuri, French, English	Hindu, Roman Catholic, other Christian, Muslim
Mayotte	NA	Mahorian (a Swahili dialect), French	Muslim, Roman Catholic
Mexico	Mestizo (Amerindian-Spanish), Amerindian, white	Spanish, various Mayan, Nahuatl, and other indigenous languages	Roman Catholic, Protestant
Micronesia, Federated States of	Nine Ethnic Micronesian and Polynesian groups	English, Trukese, Pohnpeian, Yapese, Kosrean, Ulithian, Woleaian, Nukuoro, Kapingamarangi	Roman Catholic, Protestant
Moldova	Moldovan/Romanian, Ukrainian, Russian, Gagauz, Bulgarian	Moldovan, Russian, Gagauz (a Turkish dialect)	Eastern Orthodox, Jewish, Baptist
Monaco	French, Monegasque, Italian	French, English, Italian, Monegasque	Roman Catholic
Mongolia	Mongol (mostly Khalkha), Turkic (mostly Kazakh), Chinese, Russian	Khalkha Mongol, Turkic, Russian	Buddhist Lamaist, none, Shamanist and Christian, Muslim
Montenegro	Montenegrin, Serbian, Bosniak, Albanian, Muslims, Croats, Roma	Serbian (Ijekavian dialect)	Orthodox, Muslim, Roman Catholic
Montserrat	Black, White	English	Anglican, Methodist, Roman Catholic, Pentecostal, Seventh-Day Adventist, other Christian
Morocco	Arab-Berber, Jewish	Arabic, Berber dialects, French	Muslim, Christian, Jewish
Mozambique	Makhuwa, Tsonga, Lomwe, Sena, etc., Europeans, Euro-Africans, Indians	Emakhuwa, Xichangana, Portuguese, Elomwe, Cisena, Echuwabo, other Mozambican languages	Catholic, Muslim, Zionist Christian
Namibia	Ovambo and Kavangos tribes, Herero, Damara, Nama, Caprivian, Bushmen, Baster, and Tswana, white, mixed	English, Afrikaans, German, Indigenous languages (Oshivambo, Herero, Nama)	Christian (Lutheran at least), Indigenous beliefs
Nauru	Nauruan, other Pacific Islander, Chinese, European	Nauruan (distinct Pacific Island language), English	Christian (two-thirds Protestant, one-third Roman Catholic)

(continued)

(continued)

Economy	Major ethnic groups	Major linguistic groups	Major religious groups
Nepal	Chhettri, Brahman-Hill, Magar, Tharu, Tamang, Newar, Muslim, Kami, Yadav	Nepali, Maithali, Bhojpuri, Tharu (Dagaura/Rana), Tamang, Newar, Magar, Awadhi	Hindu, Buddhist, Muslim, Kirant
Netherlands	Dutch, Turks, Moroccans, Antilleans, Surinamese, and Indonesians	Dutch, Frisian	Roman Catholic, Dutch Reformed, Calvinist, Muslim
Netherlands Antilles	Mixed black, Carib Amerindian, White, East Asian	Papiamento (Spanish-Portuguese-Dutch-English dialect), English, Dutch, Spanish, Creole	Roman Catholic, Pentecostal, Protestant, Seventh-Day Adventist, Methodist, Jehovah's Witnesses, Jewish
New Caledonia	Melanesian, European, Wallisian, Polynesian, Indonesian, Vietnamese	French, Melanesian-Polynesian dialects	Roman Catholic, Protestant
New Zealand	European, Maori, Asian, Pacific islander	English, Maori	Anglican, Roman Catholic, Presbyterian, Methodist, Pentecostal, Baptist
Nicaragua	Mestizo (Mixed Amerindian and White), White, Black, Amerindian	Spanish, Miskito	Roman Catholic, Evangelical, Moravian, Episcopal
Niger	Hausa, Djerma, Fula, Tuareg, Beri Beri (Kanouri), Arab, Toubou, and Gourmantche	French, Hausa, Djerma	Muslim, indigenous beliefs, Christian
Nigeria	Hausa and Fulani, Yoruba, Igbo (Ibo), Ijaw, Kanuri, Ibibio, Tiv	English, Hausa, Yoruba, Igbo (Ibo), Fulani	Muslim, Christian, indigenous beliefs
Niue	Niuen, Pacific Islander, European, Mixed, Asian	Niuean, a Polynesian language closely related to Tongan and Samoan; English	Ekalesia Niue (a Protestant church closely related to the London Missionary Society), Latter-Day Saints, Roman Catholic, Jehovah's Witnesses, Seventh-Day Adventist

(continued)

(continued)

Economy	Major ethnic groups	Major linguistic groups	Major religious groups
Norfolk Island	Descendants of the Bounty Mutineers, Australian, New Zealander, Polynesian	English, Norfolk a mixture of English and ancient Tahitian	Anglican, Roman Catholic, Uniting Church in Australia, Seventh-Day Adventist, Australian Christian, Jehovah's Witness
Northern Mariana Islands	Asian, Pacific Islander, Caucasian, other, Mixed	Philippine languages, Chinese, Chamorro, English, other Pacific island languages	Christian (Roman Catholic majority, traditional beliefs and taboos)
Norway	Norwegian, Sami	Bokmal Norwegian, Nynorsk Norwegian, Sami and Finnish	Church of Norway, Pentecostal, Roman Catholic, other Christian, Muslim
Oman	Arab, Baluchi, Indian, Pakistani, Sri Lankan, Bangladeshi, African	Arabic, English, Baluchi, Urdu, Indian dialects	Ibadhi Muslim, Sunni Muslim, Shi'a Muslim, Hindu
Pakistan	Punjabi, Sindhi, Pashtun (Pathan), Baloch, Muhajir	Punjabi, Sindhi, Siraiki, Pashtu, Urdu, Balochi, Hindko, Brahui, English, Burushaski	Muslim: Sunni, Shi'a, Christian, Hindu
Palau	Palauan, Filipino, Chinese, other Asian, White, Carolinian, other Micronesian	Palauan, Tobi, and Angaur, Filipino, English, Chinese, Carolinian, Japanese, other Asian	Roman Catholic, Protestant, Modekngei (indigenous to Palau), Seventh-Day Adventist, Jehovah's Witness, Latter-Day Saints
Panama	Mestizo (Mixed Amerindian and White), Amerindian and Mixed (West Indian), White, Amerindian	Spanish, English	Roman Catholic, Protestant
Papua New Guinea	Melanesian, Papuan, Negrito, Micronesian, Polynesian	Melanesian Pidgin (lingua franca), English, Motu (in Papua region)	Roman Catholic, Lutheran, Presbyterian/ Methodist/London Missionary Society, Anglican, Evangelical Alliance, Seventh-Day Adventis, other Protestant, Indigenous beliefs
Paraguay	Mestizo (Mixed Spanish and Amerindian)	Spanish, Guarani	Roman Catholic, Mennonite and other Protestant

(continued)

(continued)

Economy	Major ethnic groups	Major linguistic groups	Major religious groups
Peru	Amerindian, Mestizo (Mixed Amerindian and White), White, Black, Japanese, Chinese	Spanish, Quechua, Aymara, and a large number of minor Amazonian languages	Roman Catholic, Seventh Day Adventist, other Christian
Philippines	Tagalog, Cebuano, Ilocano, Bisaya/ Binisaya, Hiligaynon Ilonggo, Bikol, Waray	Filipino, English, Tagalog, Cebuano, Ilocano, Hiligaynon or Ilonggo, Bicol, Waray, Pampango, and Pangasinan	Roman Catholic, Evangelical, Iglesia ni Kristo, Aglipayan, other Christian, Muslim
Pitcairn Islands	Descendants of the Bounty Mutineers and their Tahitian wives	English, Pitcairnese (mixture of English and a Tahitian dialect)	Seventh-Day Adventist
Poland	Polish, German, Belarusian, Ukrainian	Polish, other and unspecified	Roman Catholic, Eastern Orthodox, Protestant
Portugal	Homogeneous Mediterranean stock; Black African descents; East Europeans	Portuguese, Mirandese	Roman Catholic, Protestant
Puerto Rico	White (mostly Spanish origin), Black, Amerindian, Asian	Spanish, English	Roman Catholic, Protestant and other
Qatar	Arab, Indian, Pakistani, Iranian	Arabic, English	Muslim
Reunion	French, African, Malagasy, Chinese, Pakistani, Indian	French, Creole widely used	Roman Catholic, Hindu, Muslim, Buddhist
Romania	Romanian, Hungarian, Roma, Ukrainian, German, Russian, Turkish	Romanian, Hungarian, German	Eastern Orthodox, Protestant, Roman Catholic, Muslim
Russia	Russian, Tatar, Ukrainian, Bashkir, Chuvash	Russian, many minority languages	Russian Orthodox, Muslim, other Christian
Rwanda	Hutu, Tutsi, Twa (Pygmoid)	Kinyarwanda, French, English, Kiswahili (Swahili)	Roman Catholic, Protestant, Adventist, Muslim, Indigenous beliefs
Saint Helena	African descent, White, Chinese	English	Anglican (majority), Baptist, Seventh-Day Adventist, Roman Catholic
Saint Kitts and Nevis	Predominantly Black; Some British, Portuguese, and Lebanese	English	Anglican, other Protestant, Roman Catholic

(continued)

(continued)

Economy	Major ethnic groups	Major linguistic groups	Major religious groups
Saint Lucia	Black, Mixed, East Indian, White	English, French patois	Roman Catholic, Seventh Day Adventist, Pentecostal, Anglican, Evangelica, other Christian, Rastafarian
Saint Pierre and Miquelon	Basques and Bretons (French fishermen)	French	Roman Catholic
Saint Vincent and the Grenadines	Black, Mixed, East Indian, Carib Amerindian	English, French patois	Anglican, Methodist, Roman Catholic, Hindu, Seventh-Day Adventist, other Protestant
Samoa	Samoan, Euronesians (European and Polynesian blood), Europeans	Samoan (Polynesian), English	Congregationalist, Roman Catholic, Methodist, Latter-Day Saints, Assembly of God, Seventh-Day Adventist, other Christian, Worship Center
San Marino	Sammarinese, Italian	Italian	Roman Catholic
Sao Tome and Principe	Mestico, Angolares (Descendants of Angolan slaves), Forros (Descendants of freed slaves), Servicais (contract laborers from Angola, Mozambique, and Cape Verde), tongas (children of servicais born on the islands), Portuguese	Portuguese	Catholic, Evangelical, New Apostolic, Adventist
Saudi Arabia	Arab, Afro-Asian	Arabic	Muslim
Senegal	Wolof, Pular, Serer, Jola, Mandinka, Soninke, European and Lebanese	French, Wolof, Pulaar, Jola, Mandinka	Muslim, Roman Catholic, Indigenous beliefs
Seychelles	Mixed French, African, Indian, Chinese, and Arab	Creole, English, other	Roman Catholic, Anglican, Seventh Day Adventist, other Christian, Hindu, Muslim
Sierra Leone	Temne, Mende, other African tribes, Creole (Krio)	English, Mende (in south), Temne (in north), Krio (English-based Creole)	Muslim, Indigenous beliefs, Christian

(continued)

(continued)

Economy	Major ethnic groups	Major linguistic groups	Major religious groups
Singapore	Chinese, Malay, Indian	Mandarin, English, Malay, Hokkien, Cantonese, Tamil, other Chinese dialects	Buddhist, Muslim, Taoist, Hindu, Catholic, other Christian
Slovakia	Slovak, Hungarian, Roma, Ruthenian/ Ukrainian	Slovak, Hungarian, Roma, Ukrainian	Roman Catholic, Protestant, Greek Catholic
Slovenia	Slovene, Serb, Croat, Bosniak	Slovenian, Serbo-Croatian	Catholic, Orthodox, other Christian, Muslim
Solomon Islands	Melanesian, Polynesian, Micronesian, other	Melanesian pidgin; English	Church of Melanesia, Roman Catholic, South Seas Evangelical, Seventh-Day Adventist, United Church, Christian Fellowship Church, other Christian
Somalia	Somali, Bantu and other non-Somali (including Arabs)	Somali, Arabic, Italian, English	Sunni Muslim
South Africa	Black African, White, colored, Indian/Asian	IsiZulu, IsiXhosa, Afrikaans, Sepedi, English, Setswana, Sesotho, Xitsonga	Zion Christian, Pentecostal/ Charismatic, Catholic, Methodist, Dutch Reformed, Anglican, other Christian, Islam
Spain	Composite of Mediterranean and Nordic types	Castilian Spanish, Catalan, Galician, Basque	Roman Catholic, other
Sri Lanka	Sinhalese, Sri Lankan Moors, Indian Tamil, Sri Lankan Tamil	Sinhala, Tamil	Buddhist, Muslim, Hindu, Christian
Sudan	Black, Arab, Beja, Foreigners	Arabic, Nubian, Ta Bedawie, dialects of Nilotic, Nilo-Hamitic, Sudanic languages, English	Sunni Muslim (in north), Indigenous beliefs, Christian
Suriname	Hindustani, Creole (Mixed White and Black), Javanese, Maroons, Amerindian, Chinese, White	Dutch, English, Sranang Tongo (or Taki-Taki), Hindustani, Javanese	Hindu, Protestant, Roman Catholic, Muslim, Indigenous beliefs
Swaziland	African, European	English, siSwati	Zionist (blend of Christianity and Indigenous ancestral worship), Roman Catholic, Muslim, Anglican, Bahai, Methodist, Mormon, Jewish

(continued)

(continued)

Economy	Major ethnic groups	Major linguistic groups	Major religious groups
Sweden	Swedes with Finnish and Sami minorities; Finns, Yugoslavs, Danes, Norwegians, Greeks, Turks	Swedish, small Sami- and Finnish-speaking minorities	Lutheran, Roman Catholic, Orthodox, Baptist, Muslim, Jewish, Buddhist
Switzerland	German, French, Italian, Romansch, other	German, French, Italian, Serbo-Croatian, Albanian, Portuguese, Spanish, English, Romansch	Roman Catholic, Protestant, Orthodox, other Christian, Muslim
Syria	Arab, Kurds, Armenians	Arabic, Kurdish, Armenian, Aramaic, Circassian; French, English	Sunni Muslim, Alawite, Druze, and other Muslim sects, Christian (various sects), Jewish
Taiwan	Taiwanese (including Hakka), mainland Chinese, aborigine	Mandarin Chinese, Taiwanese (Minnan), Hakka dialects	mixture of Buddhist, Confucian, and Taoist, Christian
Tajikistan	Tajik, Uzbek, Russian, Kyrgyz	Tajik, Russian	Sunni Muslim, Shi'a Muslim
Tanzania	Bantu (over tribes), Asian, European, and Arab	Kiswahili or Swahili, Kiunguja (Swahili in Zanzibar), English, Arabic (in Zanzibar)	mainland: Christian, Muslim, Indigenous beliefs ; Zanzibar: Muslim
Thailand	Thai, Chinese, other	Thai, English, ethnic and regional dialects	Buddhist, Muslim, Christian
Togo	Ewe, Mina, Kabre, and other native African tribes, European, Syrian-Lebanese	French, Ewe and Mina (in south), Kabye (Kabiye) and Dagomba (in north)	Indigenous beliefs, Christian, Muslim
Tokelau	Polynesian	Tokelauan (a Polynesian language), English	Congregational Christian Church, Roman Catholic
Tonga	Polynesian, Europeans	Tongan, English	Christian
Trinidad and Tobago	Indian (South Asian), African, Mixed	English, Hindi, French, Spanish, Chinese	Roman Catholic, Hindu, Anglican, Baptist, Pentecostal, other Christian, Muslim, Seventh Day Adventist
Tunisia	Arab, European, Jewish	Arabic, French	Muslim, Christian, Jewish
Turkey	Turkish, Kurdish	Turkish, Kurdish, Dimli (or Zaza), Azeri, Kabardian	Muslim (mostly Sunni), Christians, Jews
Turkmenistan	Turkmen, Uzbek, Russian	Turkmen, Russian, Uzbek	Muslim, Eastern Orthodox

(continued)

(continued)

Economy	Major ethnic groups	Major linguistic groups	Major religious groups
Turks and Caicos Islands	Black, Mixed, European, or North American	English	Baptist, Anglican, Methodist, Church of God
Tuvalu	Polynesian, Micronesian	Tuvaluan, English, Samoan, Kiribati (on the island of Nui)	Church of Tuvalu (Congregationalist), Seventh-Day Adventist, Baha'i
Uganda	Baganda, Ankole, Basoga, Iteso, Bakiga, Langi, Rwanda, Bagisu, Acholi, Lugbara, Batoro, Bunyoro, Alur, Bagwere, Bakonjo, Jopodhola, Karamojong, and Rundi	English, Ganda or Luganda, other Niger-Congo languages, Nilo-Saharan languages, Swahili, Arabic	Roman Catholic, Protestant, Muslim, Indigenous beliefs
Ukraine	Ukrainian, Russian, Belarusian, Moldovan, Crimean Tatar, Bulgarian, Hungarian, Romanian, Polish, Jewish	Ukrainian, Russian, Romanian, Polish, and Hungarian	Ukrainian Orthodox (Kiev Patri, Moscow Patri.), Orthodox, Ukrainian Greek Catholic and Autocephalous Orthodox, Protestant, Jewish
United Arab Emirates	Emirati, other Arab and Iranian, South Asian, Westerners, East Asians	Arabic, Persian, English, Hindi, Urdu	Muslim (mostly Sunni), Christian, Hindu
United Kingdom	English, Scottish, Welsh, Northern Irish, Black, Indian, Pakistani, Mixed	English, Welsh (about in Wales), Scottish form of Gaelic	Christian (Anglican, Roman Catholic, Presbyterian, Methodist), Muslim, Hindu
United States	White, Black, Asian, Amerindian and Alaska native, native Hawaiian and other Pacific Islander	English, Spanish, other Indo-European, Asian and Pacific island	Protestant, Roman Catholic, Mormon, Jewish, Muslim
Uruguay	White, Mestizo, Black, Amerindian	Spanish, Portunol, or Brazilero (Portuguese-Spanish mix on the Brazilian frontier)	Roman Catholic, Protestant, Jewish
Uzbekistan	Uzbek, Russian, Tajik, Kazakh, Karakalpak, Tatar	Uzbek, Russian, Tajik	Muslim (mostly Sunnis), Eastern Orthodox

(continued)

(continued)

Economy	Major ethnic groups	Major linguistic groups	Major religious groups
Vanuatu	Ni-Vanuatu, other	Local languages, pidgin (Bislama or Bichelama), English, French	Presbyterian, Anglican, Roman Catholic, Seventh-Day Adventist, other Christian, Indigenous beliefs
Venezuela	Spanish, Italian, Portuguese, Arab, German, African, Indigenous people	Spanish, Numerous Indigenous dialects	Roman Catholic, Protestant
Vietnam	Kinh (Viet), Tay, Thai, Muong, Khome, Hoa, Nun, Hmong	Vietnamese, English, French, Chinese, Khmer, Mon-Khmer, Malayo-Polynesian	Buddhist, Catholic, Hoa Hao, Cao Dai, Protestant, Muslim
Virgin Islands	Black, White, Asian, other	English, Spanish or Spanish Creole, French or French Creole	Baptist, Roman Catholic, Episcopalian
Wallis and Futuna	Polynesian	Wallisian (Indigenous Polynesian language), Futunian, French	Roman Catholic
West Bank	Palestinian Arab and other, Jewish	Arabic, Hebrew, English	Muslim (predominantly Sunni), Jewish, Christian
Western Sahara	Arab, Berber	Hassaniya Arabic, Moroccan Arabic	Muslim
Yemen	Arab; Afro-Arab, South Asians, Europeans	Arabic	Muslim including Shaf'i (Sunni) and Zaydi (Shi'a), Small numbers of Jewish, Christian, and Hindu
Zambia	African, European	English, Bemba, Kaonda, Lozi, Lunda, Luvale, Nyanja, Tonga	Christian, Muslim and Hindu, Indigenous beliefs
Zimbabwe	Shona, Ndebele, other African, Mixed and Asian, White	English, Shona, Sindebele (Ndebele), other minor tribal dialects	mix of Christian and Indigenous beliefs, Christian, Indigenous beliefs, Muslim

Source Guo (2009b)

Appendix B
Cultural Similarity Matrices of Countries Involved in the Research

Table B.1 Linguistic Similarity Matrix

Country or region	Brazil	China	Congo, DR	France	India	Japan	Saudi Arabia	United States
Afghanistan	0.000	0.000	0.000	0.003	0.000	0.000	0.000	0.000
Albania	0.000	0.000	0.000	0.000	0.000	0.000	0.000	0.002
Algeria	0.000	0.000	0.034	0.331	0.000	0.000	0.597	0.009
American Samoa	0.000	0.000	0.000	0.001	0.036	0.000	0.000	0.496
Andorra	0.109	0.000	0.034	0.095	0.016	0.000	0.000	0.093
Angola	0.259	0.000	0.000	0.011	0.000	0.000	0.000	0.002
Antigua and Barbuda	0.000	0.000	0.000	0.001	0.036	0.000	0.000	0.875
Argentina	0.004	0.000	0.000	0.008	0.000	0.000	0.000	0.073
Armenia	0.000	0.000	0.000	0.000	0.000	0.000	0.000	0.001
Aruba	0.000	0.000	0.000	0.005	0.036	0.000	0.000	0.164
Australia	0.010	0.017	0.002	0.024	0.036	0.002	0.008	0.873
Austria	0.006	0.000	0.000	0.004	0.000	0.000	0.000	0.010
Azerbaijan	0.000	0.000	0.000	0.000	0.000	0.000	0.000	0.002
Bahamas, The	0.000	0.000	0.034	0.105	0.036	0.000	0.000	0.883
Bahrain	0.000	0.000	0.000	0.025	0.000	0.000	0.683	0.001
Bangladesh	0.000	0.000	0.000	0.001	0.026	0.000	0.000	0.026
Barbados	0.000	0.000	0.000	0.001	0.036	0.000	0.000	0.875
Belarus	0.000	0.000	0.000	0.001	0.000	0.000	0.000	0.004
Belgium	0.010	0.000	0.034	0.354	0.000	0.000	0.016	0.026
Belize	0.006	0.000	0.000	0.005	0.036	0.000	0.000	0.588
Benin	0.000	0.000	0.034	0.133	0.000	0.000	0.000	0.007
Bermuda	0.000	0.000	0.000	0.001	0.036	0.000	0.000	0.875
Bhutan	0.000	0.000	0.000	0.000	0.000	0.000	0.000	0.000
Bolivia	0.000	0.000	0.000	0.004	0.000	0.000	0.000	0.068
Bosnia and Herzegovina	0.000	0.000	0.000	0.000	0.000	0.000	0.000	0.000
Botswana	0.000	0.000	0.000	0.001	0.036	0.000	0.000	0.286
Brazil	–	0.000	0.000	0.016	0.000	0.000	0.000	0.013
Brunei	0.000	0.095	0.000	0.001	0.033	0.002	0.000	0.038

(continued)

R. Guo, *Introduction to Intercultural Economics*, SpringerBriefs in Economics,
DOI: 10.1007/978-3-642-29276-7, © The Author(s) 2012

(continued)

Country or region	Brazil	China	Congo, DR	France	India	Japan	Saudi Arabia	United States
Bulgaria	0.000	0.000	0.027	0.030	0.000	0.000	0.000	0.008
Burkina Faso	0.000	0.000	0.034	0.056	0.000	0.000	0.000	0.007
Burundi	0.000	0.000	0.034	0.085	0.000	0.000	0.000	0.007
Cambodia	0.000	0.031	0.000	0.000	0.000	0.002	0.000	0.007
Cameroon	0.000	0.000	0.034	0.121	0.036	0.000	0.007	0.157
Canada	0.016	0.011	0.034	0.258	0.036	0.002	0.002	0.649
Cape Verde	0.975	0.000	0.000	0.011	0.000	0.000	0.000	0.002
Central African Republic	0.000	0.000	0.034	0.057	0.000	0.000	0.000	0.007
Chad	0.000	0.000	0.034	0.141	0.000	0.000	0.232	0.009
Chile	0.000	0.000	0.000	0.004	0.000	0.000	0.000	0.068
China	0.000	–	0.000	0.000	0.000	0.003	0.000	0.007
Colombia	0.000	0.000	0.000	0.005	0.001	0.000	0.000	0.069
Comoros	0.000	0.000	0.034	0.048	0.000	0.000	0.000	0.007
Congo, Dem. Rep. of the	0.000	0.000	–	0.034	0.000	0.000	0.000	0.007
Congo, Rep. of the	0.000	0.000	0.034	0.155	0.000	0.000	0.000	0.007
Costa Rica	0.000	0.002	0.000	0.005	0.020	0.002	0.000	0.090
Cote d'lvoire	0.000	0.000	0.034	0.258	0.000	0.000	0.000	0.007
Croatia	0.000	0.000	0.000	0.000	0.000	0.000	0.000	0.000
Cuba	0.000	0.000	0.000	0.004	0.000	0.000	0.000	0.068
Cyprus	0.000	0.000	0.000	0.003	0.000	0.000	0.000	0.002
Czech Republic	0.005	0.000	0.000	0.001	0.000	0.000	0.000	0.010
Denmark	0.005	0.000	0.000	0.009	0.005	0.000	0.005	0.012
Djibouti	0.000	0.000	0.034	0.100	0.000	0.000	0.104	0.009
Dominica	0.000	0.000	0.034	0.477	0.036	0.000	0.000	0.532
Dominican Republic	0.000	0.000	0.000	0.005	0.020	0.000	0.000	0.088
Ecuador	0.000	0.000	0.000	0.004	0.000	0.000	0.000	0.068
Egypt	0.000	0.000	0.004	0.030	0.000	0.000	0.950	0.006
El Salvador	0.000	0.000	0.000	0.004	0.000	0.000	0.000	0.068
Equatorial Guinea	0.000	0.000	0.000	0.000	0.000	0.000	0.000	0.000
Eritrea	0.000	0.000	0.000	0.003	0.000	0.000	0.003	0.001
Estonia	0.000	0.000	0.000	0.000	0.000	0.000	0.000	0.002
Ethiopia	0.000	0.000	0.000	0.000	0.000	0.000	0.000	0.000
Faroe Islands	0.000	0.000	0.000	0.000	0.000	0.000	0.000	0.000
Fiji	0.000	0.000	0.000	0.001	0.397	0.000	0.000	0.172
Finland	0.000	0.000	0.000	0.000	0.000	0.000	0.000	0.001
France	0.016	0.000	0.034	–	0.001	0.000	0.025	0.021
French Guiana	0.000	0.000	0.034	0.937	0.000	0.000	0.000	0.007
French Polynesia	0.000	0.029	0.034	0.409	0.000	0.002	0.000	0.012
Gabon	0.000	0.000	0.034	0.252	0.000	0.000	0.000	0.007
Gambia, The	0.000	0.000	0.000	0.000	0.000	0.000	0.000	0.000
Gaza Strip	0.000	0.000	0.000	0.025	0.000	0.000	0.950	0.002
Georgia	0.000	0.000	0.000	0.000	0.000	0.000	0.000	0.002

(continued)

(continued)

Country or region	Brazil	China	Congo, DR	France	India	Japan	Saudi Arabia	United States
Germany	0.010	0.000	0.000	0.009	0.000	0.000	0.000	0.016
Ghana	0.000	0.000	0.000	0.000	0.000	0.000	0.000	0.000
Gibraltar	0.000	0.000	0.000	0.027	0.036	0.000	0.074	0.877
Greece	0.000	0.000	0.000	0.003	0.000	0.000	0.000	0.002
Greenland	0.000	0.000	0.000	0.000	0.000	0.000	0.000	0.000
Grenada	0.000	0.000	0.000	0.001	0.036	0.000	0.000	0.875
Guadeloupe	0.000	0.000	0.034	0.937	0.000	0.000	0.000	0.007
Guam	0.004	0.015	0.000	0.001	0.036	0.007	0.000	0.620
Guatemala	0.000	0.000	0.000	0.004	0.000	0.000	0.000	0.068
Guernsey	0.000	0.000	0.000	0.001	0.036	0.000	0.000	0.875
Guinea	0.000	0.000	0.034	0.077	0.000	0.000	0.000	0.007
Guinea-Bissau	0.145	0.000	0.000	0.011	0.000	0.000	0.000	0.002
Guyana	0.000	0.000	0.000	0.001	0.036	0.000	0.000	0.875
Haiti	0.000	0.000	0.034	0.937	0.000	0.000	0.000	0.007
Honduras	0.000	0.000	0.000	0.005	0.002	0.000	0.000	0.070
Hong Kong	0.001	0.766	0.000	0.001	0.036	0.002	0.000	0.212
Hungary	0.004	0.000	0.000	0.000	0.000	0.000	0.000	0.006
Iceland	0.000	0.000	0.000	0.000	0.000	0.000	0.000	0.000
India	0.000	0.000	0.000	0.001	–	0.000	0.000	0.037
Indonesia	0.000	0.000	0.000	0.000	0.000	0.000	0.000	0.000
Iran	0.000	0.000	0.000	0.015	0.000	0.000	0.012	0.002
Iraq	0.000	0.000	0.000	0.025	0.000	0.000	0.771	0.001
Ireland	0.000	0.000	0.000	0.001	0.036	0.000	0.000	0.741
Isle of Man	0.000	0.000	0.000	0.001	0.036	0.000	0.000	0.875
Israel	0.000	0.000	0.000	0.025	0.000	0.000	0.180	0.003
Italy	0.009	0.000	0.005	0.010	0.000	0.000	0.000	0.016
Jamaica	0.000	0.000	0.000	0.001	0.056	0.000	0.000	0.877
Japan	0.004	0.003	0.000	0.001	0.001	–	0.000	0.006
Jersey	0.000	0.000	0.000	0.001	0.036	0.000	0.000	0.875
Jordan	0.000	0.000	0.000	0.025	0.000	0.000	0.950	0.002
Kazakstan	0.006	0.009	0.000	0.000	0.000	0.005	0.000	0.010
Kenya	0.000	0.000	0.000	0.003	0.036	0.000	0.001	0.045
Kiribati	0.000	0.000	0.000	0.000	0.000	0.000	0.000	0.000
Korea, North	0.000	0.003	0.000	0.000	0.000	0.007	0.000	0.004
Korea, South	0.000	0.003	0.000	0.000	0.000	0.006	0.000	0.004
Kuwait	0.000	0.000	0.000	0.025	0.000	0.000	0.781	0.001
Kyrgyzstan	0.006	0.001	0.000	0.000	0.000	0.000	0.000	0.007
Laos	0.000	0.000	0.000	0.000	0.000	0.000	0.000	0.000
Latvia	0.000	0.000	0.000	0.001	0.000	0.000	0.000	0.004
Lebanon	0.000	0.000	0.034	0.219	0.000	0.000	0.749	0.009
Lesotho	0.000	0.000	0.000	0.001	0.036	0.000	0.000	0.166
Liberia	0.000	0.000	0.000	0.001	0.036	0.000	0.000	0.520
Libya	0.000	0.000	0.000	0.025	0.000	0.000	0.950	0.001
Liechtenstein	0.010	0.000	0.000	0.008	0.000	0.000	0.000	0.011

(continued)

(continued)

Country or region	Brazil	China	Congo, DR	France	India	Japan	Saudi Arabia	United States
Lithuania	0.000	0.000	0.000	0.001	0.000	0.000	0.000	0.004
Luxembourg	0.131	0.000	0.034	0.057	0.012	0.000	0.000	0.042
Macau	0.024	0.921	0.000	0.013	0.005	0.002	0.000	0.012
Macedonia	0.000	0.000	0.000	0.003	0.000	0.000	0.000	0.001
Madagascar	0.000	0.000	0.034	0.091	0.000	0.000	0.000	0.007
Malawi	0.000	0.006	0.000	0.001	0.036	0.000	0.000	0.048
Malaysia	0.000	0.070	0.000	0.001	0.036	0.002	0.000	0.251
Maldives	0.000	0.000	0.000	0.000	0.000	0.000	0.000	0.000
Mali	0.000	0.000	0.034	0.051	0.000	0.000	0.009	0.009
Malta	0.000	0.000	0.000	0.001	0.021	0.000	0.000	0.021
Marshall Islands	0.000	0.000	0.000	0.001	0.036	0.000	0.000	0.500
Martinique	0.000	0.000	0.034	0.937	0.000	0.000	0.000	0.007
Mauritania	0.000	0.000	0.034	0.055	0.000	0.000	0.000	0.007
Mauritius	0.000	0.004	0.034	0.742	0.014	0.002	0.000	0.014
Mayotte	0.000	0.000	0.034	0.203	0.000	0.000	0.000	0.007
Mexico	0.000	0.000	0.000	0.004	0.000	0.000	0.000	0.068
Micronesia	0.000	0.000	0.000	0.001	0.005	0.000	0.000	0.005
Moldova	0.000	0.000	0.000	0.000	0.000	0.000	0.000	0.002
Monaco	0.004	0.000	0.034	0.425	0.036	0.000	0.000	0.077
Mongolia	0.000	0.005	0.000	0.000	0.000	0.000	0.000	0.000
Morocco	0.000	0.000	0.000	0.025	0.000	0.000	0.650	0.001
Mozambique	0.012	0.006	0.000	0.011	0.000	0.000	0.000	0.002
Myanmar	0.000	0.000	0.000	0.000	0.000	0.000	0.000	0.000
Namibia	0.006	0.000	0.000	0.001	0.036	0.000	0.000	0.084
Nauru	0.000	0.044	0.000	0.001	0.036	0.000	0.000	0.523
Nepal	0.000	0.000	0.000	0.000	0.029	0.000	0.000	0.001
Netherlands, The	0.000	0.000	0.000	0.013	0.000	0.000	0.009	0.002
Netherlands Antilles	0.000	0.000	0.000	0.001	0.036	0.000	0.000	0.079
New Caledonia	0.000	0.000	0.034	0.343	0.000	0.000	0.000	0.009
New Zealand	0.000	0.000	0.000	0.001	0.036	0.000	0.000	0.875
Nicaragua	0.000	0.000	0.000	0.001	0.009	0.000	0.000	0.009
Niger	0.000	0.000	0.034	0.131	0.000	0.000	0.000	0.007
Nigeria	0.000	0.000	0.000	0.003	0.036	0.000	0.001	0.256
Northern Mariana	0.004	0.039	0.000	0.001	0.036	0.007	0.000	0.484
Norway	0.000	0.000	0.000	0.001	0.005	0.000	0.000	0.006
Oman	0.000	0.000	0.000	0.025	0.000	0.000	0.767	0.001
Pakistan	0.000	0.000	0.000	0.001	0.036	0.000	0.000	0.105
Palau	0.000	0.009	0.000	0.001	0.036	0.002	0.000	0.505
Panama	0.000	0.003	0.000	0.005	0.036	0.002	0.000	0.212
Papua New Guinea	0.000	0.000	0.000	0.001	0.009	0.000	0.000	0.009
Paraguay	0.037	0.000	0.000	0.015	0.000	0.000	0.000	0.073
Peru	0.000	0.000	0.000	0.004	0.000	0.000	0.000	0.068
Philippines	0.000	0.001	0.000	0.001	0.036	0.001	0.000	0.343
Poland	0.006	0.000	0.000	0.001	0.000	0.000	0.000	0.009

(continued)

(continued)

Country or region	Brazil	China	Congo, DR	France	India	Japan	Saudi Arabia	United States
Portugal	0.975	0.000	0.000	0.011	0.000	0.000	0.000	0.002
Puerto Rico	0.000	0.000	0.000	0.005	0.005	0.000	0.000	0.073
Qatar	0.000	0.000	0.000	0.025	0.000	0.000	0.403	0.001
Reunion	0.000	0.020	0.034	0.812	0.000	0.002	0.000	0.012
Romania	0.004	0.000	0.000	0.001	0.000	0.000	0.000	0.008
Russia	0.002	0.001	0.000	0.000	0.000	0.000	0.000	0.005
Rwanda	0.000	0.000	0.034	0.064	0.000	0.000	0.000	0.007
St. Kitts and Nevis	0.000	0.000	0.000	0.001	0.036	0.000	0.000	0.875
St. Lucia	0.000	0.000	0.000	0.001	0.036	0.000	0.000	0.207
St. Vincent and the Grenadines	0.000	0.000	0.000	0.001	0.036	0.000	0.000	0.875
Samoa	0.000	0.000	0.000	0.001	0.006	0.000	0.000	0.006
San Marino	0.000	0.000	0.000	0.000	0.000	0.000	0.000	0.000
Sao Tome and Principe	0.861	0.000	0.007	0.019	0.000	0.000	0.000	0.009
Saudi Arabia	0.000	0.000	0.000	0.025	0.000	0.000	–	0.001
Senegal	0.000	0.000	0.034	0.048	0.000	0.000	0.000	0.007
Seychelles	0.000	0.000	0.034	0.812	0.036	0.000	0.000	0.180
Sierra Leone	0.000	0.000	0.000	0.001	0.036	0.000	0.000	0.458
Singapore	0.000	0.563	0.000	0.001	0.036	0.002	0.000	0.277
Slovakia	0.001	0.000	0.000	0.001	0.000	0.000	0.000	0.003
Slovenia	0.000	0.000	0.000	0.000	0.000	0.000	0.000	0.001
Solomon Islands	0.000	0.000	0.000	0.001	0.019	0.000	0.000	0.019
Somalia	0.000	0.000	0.000	0.000	0.000	0.000	0.000	0.000
South Africa	0.000	0.000	0.000	0.001	0.036	0.000	0.000	0.091
Spain	0.000	0.000	0.000	0.004	0.000	0.000	0.000	0.068
Sri Lanka	0.000	0.000	0.000	0.001	0.036	0.000	0.000	0.103
Sudan, The	0.000	0.000	0.000	0.025	0.000	0.000	0.494	0.001
Suriname	0.000	0.000	0.000	0.000	0.000	0.000	0.000	0.000
Swaziland	0.000	0.000	0.000	0.000	0.000	0.000	0.000	0.000
Sweden	0.005	0.000	0.000	0.017	0.004	0.000	0.008	0.020
Switzerland	0.010	0.000	0.034	0.197	0.000	0.000	0.000	0.019
Syria	0.000	0.000	0.000	0.025	0.000	0.000	0.900	0.001
Taiwan	0.000	0.921	0.000	0.000	0.000	0.002	0.000	0.005
Tajikistan	0.000	0.000	0.000	0.000	0.000	0.000	0.000	0.001
Tanzania	0.000	0.002	0.000	0.001	0.016	0.000	0.000	0.016
Thailand	0.000	0.121	0.000	0.000	0.000	0.002	0.000	0.006
Togo	0.000	0.000	0.034	0.146	0.000	0.000	0.000	0.007
Tonga	0.000	0.000	0.000	0.000	0.000	0.000	0.000	0.000
Trinidad and Tobago	0.000	0.000	0.000	0.001	0.063	0.000	0.000	0.030
Tunisia	0.000	0.000	0.000	0.025	0.000	0.000	0.950	0.001
Turkey	0.000	0.000	0.000	0.017	0.000	0.000	0.014	0.002
Turkmenistan	0.000	0.001	0.000	0.000	0.000	0.000	0.000	0.002
Tuvalu	0.000	0.000	0.000	0.000	0.000	0.000	0.000	0.000
Uganda	0.000	0.000	0.000	0.001	0.053	0.000	0.000	0.071

(continued)

(continued)

Country or region	Brazil	China	Congo, DR	France	India	Japan	Saudi Arabia	United States
Ukraine	0.000	0.000	0.000	0.001	0.000	0.000	0.000	0.003
United Arab Emirates	0.000	0.000	0.000	0.025	0.000	0.000	0.419	0.001
United Kingdom	0.000	0.000	0.000	0.001	0.036	0.000	0.000	0.875
United States	0.013	0.008	0.034	0.021	0.037	0.005	0.001	–
Uruguay	0.000	0.000	0.000	0.004	0.000	0.000	0.000	0.068
Uzbekistan	0.000	0.003	0.000	0.003	0.000	0.005	0.000	0.004
Vanuatu	0.000	0.000	0.034	0.143	0.036	0.000	0.000	0.856
Venezuela	0.000	0.000	0.000	0.004	0.000	0.000	0.000	0.068
Vietnam	0.000	0.023	0.005	0.005	0.000	0.002	0.000	0.012
Virgin Islands (US)	0.000	0.000	0.031	0.036	0.036	0.000	0.000	0.881
West Bank	0.000	0.000	0.000	0.025	0.000	0.000	0.922	0.002
Western Sahara	0.000	0.000	0.000	0.025	0.000	0.000	0.950	0.001
Yemen	0.000	0.000	0.000	0.025	0.000	0.000	0.950	0.001
Yugoslavia	0.000	0.000	0.000	0.000	0.000	0.000	0.000	0.002
Zambia	0.000	0.000	0.000	0.001	0.036	0.000	0.000	0.132
Zimbabwe	0.000	0.000	0.000	0.001	0.036	0.000	0.000	0.322

Note Languages included in the calculation are Amharic, Arabic, Armenian, Bengali, Chinese, Czech, Danish, Dutch, English, Finnish, French, Greek, Hebrew, Hindi, Hungarian, Italian, Japanese, Kazak, Korean, Kyrgyz, Miao, Mongol, Norwegian, Polish, Portuguese, Punjabi, Romanian, Samoan, Serbo-Croatian, Slovak, Spanish, Swedish, Tai, Tajik, Thai, Turkish, Uighur, Ukrainian, Vietnamese, Yao, and Yiddish
Source Calculated based on Eq. 7.3 and *Britannica Book for the Year 1996*

Table B.2 Religious Similarity Matrix

Country or region	Brazil	China	Congo, DR	France	India	Japan	Saudi Arabia	USA
Afghanistan	0.000	0.015	0.014	0.055	0.111	0.000	0.988	0.016
Albania	0.052	0.066	0.066	0.107	0.146	0.007	0.702	0.091
Algeria	0.000	0.015	0.014	0.055	0.111	0.000	0.988	0.016
Andorra	0.922	0.059	0.860	0.781	0.035	0.007	0.000	0.812
Angola	0.698	0.059	0.698	0.698	0.035	0.007	0.000	0.698
Antigua and Barbuda	0.846	0.059	0.846	0.781	0.035	0.007	0.000	0.812
Argentina	0.952	0.074	0.874	0.803	0.050	0.007	0.015	0.834
Armenia	0.000	0.000	0.000	0.000	0.000	0.000	0.000	0.024
Australia	0.703	0.059	0.703	0.703	0.035	0.007	0.000	0.727
Austria	0.828	0.059	0.828	0.781	0.035	0.007	0.000	0.812
Azerbaijan	0.000	0.015	0.014	0.055	0.111	0.000	0.933	0.037
Bahamas	0.941	0.059	0.860	0.781	0.035	0.007	0.000	0.812
Bahrain	0.000	0.015	0.014	0.055	0.111	0.000	0.823	0.016
Bangladesh	0.000	0.015	0.014	0.055	0.216	0.000	0.883	0.019
Barbados	0.672	0.059	0.672	0.672	0.035	0.007	0.000	0.672
Belarus	0.178	0.059	0.178	0.178	0.035	0.007	0.000	0.201
Belgium	0.879	0.059	0.860	0.781	0.035	0.007	0.000	0.812

(continued)

(continued)

Country or region	Brazil	China	Congo, DR	France	India	Japan	Saudi Arabia	USA
Belize	0.921	0.059	0.860	0.781	0.035	0.007	0.000	0.812
Benin	0.210	0.074	0.224	0.265	0.146	0.007	0.120	0.226
Bhutan	0.000	0.085	0.000	0.000	0.260	0.409	0.000	0.011
Bolivia	0.955	0.059	0.860	0.781	0.035	0.007	0.000	0.812
Bosnia and Herzegovina	0.135	0.074	0.149	0.190	0.146	0.007	0.401	0.174
Botswana	0.440	0.059	0.440	0.440	0.035	0.007	0.000	0.440
Brazil	–	0.059	0.860	0.781	0.035	0.007	0.000	0.812
Brunei Darussalam	0.000	0.015	0.014	0.055	0.111	0.000	0.672	0.016
Bulgaria	0.000	0.015	0.014	0.055	0.111	0.000	0.131	0.039
Burkina Faso	0.100	0.074	0.114	0.155	0.146	0.007	0.500	0.116
Burundi	0.813	0.059	0.813	0.781	0.035	0.007	0.000	0.812
Cambodia	0.000	0.099	0.014	0.021	0.028	0.409	0.021	0.024
Cameroon	0.524	0.074	0.538	0.579	0.146	0.007	0.217	0.540
Canada	0.816	0.075	0.825	0.800	0.062	0.013	0.009	0.857
Cape Verde	0.955	0.059	0.860	0.781	0.035	0.007	0.000	0.812
Central African Rep.	0.426	0.074	0.440	0.481	0.146	0.007	0.150	0.442
Chad	0.348	0.074	0.362	0.403	0.146	0.007	0.540	0.364
Chile	0.892	0.059	0.860	0.781	0.035	0.007	0.000	0.812
China	0.059	–	0.073	0.074	0.057	0.092	0.015	0.082
Colombia	0.919	0.059	0.860	0.781	0.035	0.007	0.000	0.812
Comoros	0.007	0.021	0.021	0.062	0.117	0.007	0.988	0.023
Congo, Dem. Rep. of the	0.860	0.073	–	0.795	0.049	0.007	0.014	0.826
Congo, Rep. of the	0.653	0.074	0.666	0.672	0.054	0.007	0.019	0.668
Costa Rica	0.813	0.059	0.813	0.781	0.035	0.007	0.000	0.812
Cote d'Ivoire	0.260	0.074	0.274	0.315	0.146	0.007	0.387	0.276
Croatia	0.727	0.072	0.740	0.740	0.048	0.007	0.013	0.764
Cuba	0.000	0.015	0.014	0.055	0.111	0.000	0.395	0.016
Cyprus	0.035	0.050	0.049	0.090	0.145	0.007	0.233	0.074
Czech Republic	0.430	0.059	0.430	0.430	0.035	0.007	0.000	0.432
Denmark	0.871	0.059	0.860	0.781	0.035	0.007	0.000	0.812
Djibouti	0.027	0.042	0.041	0.082	0.138	0.007	0.973	0.043
Dominica	0.865	0.059	0.860	0.781	0.035	0.007	0.000	0.812
Dominican Republic	0.882	0.059	0.860	0.781	0.035	0.007	0.000	0.812
Ecuador	0.925	0.059	0.860	0.781	0.035	0.007	0.000	0.812
Egypt	0.010	0.025	0.024	0.065	0.121	0.007	0.890	0.049
El Salvador	0.853	0.059	0.853	0.781	0.035	0.007	0.000	0.812
Equatorial Guinea	0.932	0.059	0.860	0.781	0.035	0.007	0.000	0.812
Eritrea	0.000	0.015	0.014	0.055	0.111	0.000	0.694	0.039
Estonia	0.137	0.059	0.137	0.137	0.035	0.007	0.000	0.161
Ethiopia	0.083	0.074	0.097	0.138	0.146	0.007	0.301	0.122
Fiji	0.530	0.074	0.543	0.584	0.495	0.007	0.078	0.549
Finland	0.858	0.059	0.858	0.781	0.035	0.007	0.000	0.812
France	0.781	0.074	0.795	–	0.090	0.007	0.055	0.807
French Guiana	0.546	0.059	0.546	0.546	0.035	0.007	0.000	0.546

(continued)

(continued)

Country or region	Brazil	China	Congo, DR	France	India	Japan	Saudi Arabia	USA
French Polynesia	0.899	0.059	0.860	0.781	0.035	0.007	0.000	0.812
Gabon	0.681	0.059	0.681	0.681	0.035	0.007	0.000	0.681
Gambia	0.000	0.015	0.014	0.055	0.111	0.000	0.952	0.016
Georgia	0.000	0.015	0.014	0.055	0.110	0.000	0.110	0.039
Germany	0.767	0.074	0.781	0.789	0.056	0.007	0.021	0.783
Ghana	0.641	0.074	0.655	0.696	0.146	0.007	0.144	0.657
Greece	0.000	0.013	0.013	0.013	0.013	0.000	0.013	0.037
Grenada	0.673	0.059	0.673	0.673	0.035	0.007	0.000	0.673
Guadeloupe	0.814	0.059	0.814	0.781	0.035	0.007	0.000	0.812
Guatemala	0.955	0.059	0.860	0.781	0.035	0.007	0.000	0.812
Guinea	0.043	0.058	0.057	0.098	0.146	0.007	0.868	0.059
Guinea-Bissau	0.051	0.066	0.065	0.106	0.146	0.007	0.297	0.067
Guyana	0.389	0.074	0.403	0.444	0.466	0.007	0.091	0.409
Haiti	0.914	0.059	0.860	0.781	0.035	0.007	0.000	0.812
Honduras	0.955	0.059	0.860	0.781	0.035	0.007	0.000	0.812
Hong Kong	0.085	0.144	0.085	0.085	0.042	0.416	0.000	0.093
Hungary	0.886	0.059	0.860	0.781	0.035	0.007	0.000	0.812
Iceland	0.904	0.059	0.860	0.781	0.035	0.007	0.000	0.812
India	0.035	0.057	0.049	0.090	–	0.014	0.111	0.062
Indonesia	0.000	0.025	0.014	0.055	0.136	0.010	0.872	0.051
Iran, Islamic Rep. of	0.000	0.015	0.014	0.055	0.111	0.000	0.988	0.016
Iraq	0.030	0.045	0.044	0.085	0.141	0.007	0.970	0.046
Ireland	0.918	0.059	0.860	0.781	0.035	0.007	0.000	0.812
Israel	0.000	0.015	0.014	0.065	0.111	0.000	0.148	0.039
Italy	0.817	0.072	0.830	0.793	0.047	0.007	0.012	0.825
Jamaica	0.528	0.059	0.528	0.528	0.035	0.007	0.000	0.528
Japan	0.007	0.092	0.007	0.007	0.014	–	0.000	0.015
Jordan	0.035	0.050	0.049	0.090	0.146	0.007	0.965	0.051
Kazakstan	0.021	0.036	0.035	0.076	0.132	0.007	0.470	0.061
Kenya	0.601	0.074	0.615	0.656	0.094	0.007	0.059	0.617
Kiribati	0.537	0.059	0.537	0.537	0.035	0.007	0.000	0.537
Korea, DPR.	0.000	0.000	0.000	0.000	0.000	0.000	0.000	0.000
Korea, Republic	0.241	0.144	0.241	0.241	0.042	0.250	0.000	0.248
Kuwait	0.000	0.015	0.014	0.055	0.111	0.000	0.850	0.016
Kyrgyzstan	0.000	0.015	0.014	0.055	0.111	0.000	0.700	0.039
Lao PDR	0.000	0.085	0.000	0.000	0.007	0.409	0.000	0.008
Latvia	0.295	0.059	0.295	0.295	0.035	0.007	0.000	0.319
Lebanon	0.236	0.074	0.250	0.291	0.146	0.007	0.552	0.275
Lesotho	0.700	0.059	0.700	0.700	0.035	0.007	0.000	0.700
Liberia	0.677	0.074	0.691	0.732	0.146	0.007	0.138	0.693
Libyan Arab Jamahiriya	0.000	0.015	0.014	0.055	0.111	0.000	0.970	0.016
Lithuania	0.720	0.059	0.720	0.720	0.035	0.007	0.000	0.743
Luxembourg	0.952	0.059	0.860	0.781	0.035	0.007	0.000	0.812
Macau	0.000	0.085	0.000	0.000	0.007	0.169	0.000	0.008

(continued)

(continued)

Country or region	Brazil	China	Congo, DR	France	India	Japan	Saudi Arabia	USA
Macedonia, The FYR of	0.000	0.015	0.014	0.055	0.111	0.000	0.302	0.039
Madagascar	0.410	0.074	0.424	0.465	0.105	0.007	0.070	0.426
Malawi	0.484	0.074	0.498	0.539	0.146	0.007	0.200	0.500
Malaysia	0.064	0.159	0.078	0.119	0.223	0.180	0.529	0.091
Maldives	0.000	0.015	0.014	0.055	0.111	0.000	0.988	0.016
Mali	0.010	0.025	0.024	0.065	0.121	0.007	0.899	0.026
Malta	0.933	0.059	0.860	0.781	0.035	0.007	0.000	0.812
Martinique	0.875	0.059	0.860	0.781	0.035	0.007	0.000	0.812
Mauritania	0.000	0.015	0.014	0.055	0.111	0.000	0.988	0.016
Mauritius	0.272	0.074	0.286	0.327	0.654	0.007	0.167	0.291
Mexico	0.955	0.059	0.860	0.781	0.035	0.007	0.000	0.812
Moldova, Rep. of	0.000	0.000	0.000	0.000	0.000	0.000	0.000	0.024
Monaco	0.813	0.059	0.813	0.781	0.035	0.007	0.000	0.812
Mongolia	0.000	0.099	0.014	0.038	0.045	0.409	0.038	0.024
Morocco	0.000	0.015	0.014	0.055	0.111	0.000	0.988	0.016
Mozambique	0.248	0.074	0.262	0.303	0.146	0.007	0.130	0.264
Myanmar	0.049	0.149	0.063	0.087	0.086	0.416	0.038	0.076
Namibia	0.809	0.059	0.809	0.781	0.035	0.007	0.000	0.809
Nepal	0.000	0.093	0.014	0.035	0.845	0.078	0.035	0.027
Netherlands	0.540	0.074	0.738	0.581	0.076	0.007	0.041	0.556
Netherlands Antilles	0.738	0.059	0.554	0.738	0.035	0.007	0.000	0.738
New Caledonia	0.756	0.059	0.756	0.756	0.035	0.007	0.000	0.756
New Zealand	0.616	0.059	0.616	0.616	0.035	0.007	0.000	0.616
Nicaragua	0.918	0.059	0.860	0.781	0.035	0.007	0.000	0.812
Niger	0.000	0.015	0.014	0.055	0.111	0.000	0.870	0.016
Nigeria	0.348	0.074	0.362	0.403	0.146	0.007	0.430	0.364
Norway	0.882	0.059	0.860	0.781	0.035	0.007	0.000	0.812
Oman	0.040	0.054	0.054	0.095	0.221	0.007	0.876	0.059
Pakistan	0.020	0.035	0.034	0.075	0.148	0.007	0.950	0.039
Palau	0.647	0.059	0.647	0.647	0.035	0.007	0.000	0.647
Panama	0.945	0.059	0.860	0.781	0.035	0.007	0.000	0.812
Papua New Guinea	0.922	0.059	0.860	0.781	0.035	0.007	0.000	0.812
Paraguay	0.955	0.059	0.860	0.781	0.035	0.007	0.000	0.812
Peru	0.955	0.059	0.860	0.781	0.035	0.007	0.000	0.812
Philippines	0.907	0.074	0.874	0.826	0.081	0.007	0.046	0.828
Poland	0.907	0.059	0.860	0.781	0.035	0.007	0.000	0.827
Portugal	0.923	0.059	0.860	0.781	0.035	0.007	0.000	0.812
Puerto Rico	0.932	0.059	0.860	0.781	0.035	0.007	0.000	0.812
Qatar	0.000	0.015	0.014	0.055	0.111	0.000	0.950	0.016
Reunion	0.882	0.074	0.874	0.836	0.146	0.007	0.118	0.828
Romania	0.050	0.050	0.050	0.050	0.035	0.007	0.000	0.074
Russian Federation	0.009	0.024	0.023	0.068	0.109	0.007	0.100	0.053
Rwanda	0.740	0.070	0.751	0.751	0.045	0.007	0.010	0.751
Samoa	0.846	0.059	0.846	0.781	0.035	0.007	0.000	0.812

(continued)

(continued)

Country or region	Brazil	China	Congo, DR	France	India	Japan	Saudi Arabia	USA
San Marino	0.885	0.059	0.860	0.781	0.035	0.007	0.000	0.812
Sao Tome and Principe	0.955	0.059	0.860	0.781	0.035	0.007	0.000	0.812
Saudi Arabia	0.000	0.015	0.014	0.055	0.111	0.000	–	0.016
Senegal	0.020	0.035	0.034	0.075	0.131	0.007	0.920	0.036
Seychelles	0.885	0.059	0.860	0.781	0.035	0.007	0.000	0.812
Sierra Leone	0.100	0.074	0.114	0.155	0.146	0.007	0.600	0.116
Singapore	0.129	0.159	0.143	0.184	0.186	0.416	0.149	0.156
Slovakia	0.667	0.059	0.667	0.667	0.035	0.007	0.000	0.667
Slovenia	0.827	0.059	0.827	0.781	0.035	0.007	0.000	0.812
Solomon Islands	0.949	0.059	0.860	0.781	0.035	0.007	0.000	0.812
Somalia	0.000	0.015	0.014	0.055	0.111	0.000	0.988	0.016
South Africa	0.943	0.074	0.874	0.809	0.085	0.007	0.024	0.838
Spain	0.667	0.071	0.679	0.679	0.047	0.007	0.011	0.679
Sri Lanka	0.069	0.159	0.083	0.124	0.273	0.416	0.076	0.096
St. Kitts and Nevis	0.333	0.059	0.333	0.333	0.035	0.007	0.000	0.333
St. Lucia	0.791	0.059	0.791	0.781	0.035	0.007	0.000	0.791
St. Vincent and the Grenadines	0.741	0.059	0.741	0.741	0.035	0.007	0.000	0.741
Sudan	0.091	0.074	0.105	0.146	0.146	0.007	0.730	0.107
Suriname	0.373	0.074	0.387	0.428	0.419	0.007	0.196	0.392
Swaziland	0.670	0.059	0.670	0.670	0.035	0.007	0.000	0.670
Sweden	0.865	0.059	0.860	0.781	0.035	0.007	0.000	0.812
Switzerland	0.861	0.059	0.860	0.781	0.035	0.007	0.000	0.812
Syrian Arab Republic	0.055	0.070	0.069	0.110	0.146	0.007	0.860	0.071
Taiwan	0.034	0.121	0.037	0.037	0.044	0.235	0.002	0.045
Tajikistan	0.000	0.015	0.014	0.055	0.111	0.000	0.850	0.031
Tanzania	0.300	0.074	0.314	0.355	0.146	0.007	0.350	0.316
Thailand	0.005	0.105	0.019	0.046	0.053	0.414	0.040	0.029
Togo	0.283	0.074	0.297	0.338	0.146	0.007	0.121	0.299
Tonga	0.158	0.059	0.158	0.158	0.035	0.007	0.000	0.158
Trinidad and Tobago	0.591	0.074	0.605	0.646	0.331	0.007	0.059	0.610
Tunisia	0.000	0.015	0.014	0.055	0.111	0.000	0.988	0.016
Turkey	0.000	0.015	0.014	0.055	0.111	0.000	0.988	0.016
Turkmenistan	0.000	0.015	0.014	0.055	0.111	0.000	0.870	0.039
Uganda	0.612	0.074	0.626	0.667	0.101	0.007	0.066	0.627
Ukraine	0.117	0.059	0.117	0.126	0.035	0.007	0.000	0.150
United Arab Emirates	0.000	0.015	0.014	0.055	0.111	0.000	0.961	0.016
United Kingdom	0.643	0.074	0.657	0.663	0.061	0.007	0.014	0.677
United States of America	0.812	0.082	0.874	0.807	0.062	0.015	0.016	–
Uruguay	0.786	0.059	0.786	0.781	0.035	0.007	0.000	0.786
Uzbekistan	0.000	0.015	0.014	0.055	0.111	0.000	0.880	0.026
Vanuatu	0.500	0.059	0.500	0.500	0.035	0.007	0.000	0.524
Venezuela	0.922	0.059	0.860	0.781	0.035	0.007	0.000	0.812
Viet Nam	0.087	0.144	0.087	0.087	0.042	0.416	0.000	0.095

(continued)

(continued)

Country or region	Brazil	China	Congo, DR	France	India	Japan	Saudi Arabia	USA
Yemen	0.000	0.015	0.014	0.055	0.111	0.000	0.988	0.016
Yugoslavia	0.058	0.073	0.072	0.113	0.169	0.007	0.248	0.098
Zambia	0.398	0.059	0.398	0.398	0.035	0.007	0.000	0.398
Zimbabwe	0.417	0.059	0.417	0.417	0.035	0.007	0.000	0.417

Note Religions included in the calculation are Christian, Eastern Orthodox, Jewish, Muslim, Buddhist, Chinese folk-religion (a mixture of Confucianism and Taoism), Hindu, Sikh, and Bahai
Source Calculated based on Eq. 3.3 and *Britannica Book for the Year 1996*

MIX
Papier aus verantwortungsvollen Quellen
Paper from responsible sources
FSC® C105338

If you have any concerns about our products,
you can contact us on
ProductSafety@springernature.com

In case Publisher is established outside the EU,
the EU authorized representative is:
Springer Nature Customer Service Center GmbH
Europaplatz 3, 69115 Heidelberg, Germany

Printed by Libri Plureos GmbH
in Hamburg, Germany